BLEEDING PINSTRIPES

FILIP BONDY

FOREWORD BY DAVID CONE

www.SportsPublishingLLC.com

ISBN: 1-58261-769-4

Publishers: Peter L. Bannon and Joseph J. Bannon Sr.
Senior managing editor: Susan M. Moyer
Acquisitions editor: Mike Pearson
Developmental editor: Elisa Bock Laird
Art director: K. Jeffrey Higgerson
Dust jacket design: Dustin Hubbart
Project manager: Kathryn R. Holleman
Imaging: Heidi Norsen
Photo editor: Erin Linden-Levy
Vice president of sales and marketing: Kevin King
Media and promotions managers: Courtney Hainline (regional), Randy Fouts (national), Maurey Williamson (print)

Printed in the United States of America

Sports Publishing L.L.C.
804 North Neil Street
Champaign, IL 61820

Phone: 1-877-424-2665
Fax: 217-363-2073
Web site: www.SportsPublishingLLC.com

TO DOMINIK, THE LITTLEST MISCHIEF MAKER.

CONTENTS

FOREWORD

We couldn't miss them out there whenever we were down on the field at Yankee Stadium. We couldn't ignore them. Just in case we failed to notice their screams and their banners, the Bleacher Creatures always made sure they grabbed our attention with their unique roll call. The roll call came at the very start of each game and demanded a tip of the cap or glove from each Yankee on the field. It was amazing how persistent and passionate the fans were about their little ritual. As a starting pitcher on the team, I always felt the crowd in right field was challenging the players to come prepared every night. The Bleacher Creatures were saying, "We're here. We're doing the roll call. Now you guys make sure you show up."

You could hear them clearly, like they were right behind you in the infield. At first, I thought maybe they'd stop doing the roll call after a few games. But they kept it up, and it caught on as a nightly affair. All the players, even our old-school coach Don Zimmer, found ourselves waving to the fans at one time or another. It was a little harder for a pitcher to acknowledge the chant when his name was called. The center fielder and the third baseman had some dead time to spare. But the pitcher, this was his day and he was wrapped up in the game from the start. David Wells was the first pitcher to acknowledge the roll call, and I give him a lot of credit for that. The fans loved him for it. I followed suit when I saw their great reaction.

The Creatures would start things off, set the tone, and then the rest of the crowd would pick up on all the emotion. That's what I took away most from the New York fans, and from the Bleacher Creatures: their consistent level of passion. They were there for every game, whether it was against Boston or Detroit. The opponent almost didn't matter. There was a certain edge and a toughness to them, and the other dugouts noticed. It was part of what created our home-field advantage in the Bronx.

We always felt as if we were in the center of the baseball universe at Yankee Stadium. The fans made it seem that way. I remember pitching there on so many big occasions: the day Joe DiMaggio died, the day Mickey Mantle died, and most notably on Yogi Berra Day—his return to the stadium and reconciliation with George Steinbrenner. That was July 18, 1999, the day I pitched my perfect game. Afterward I came out from the dugout for a curtain call, and I made sure I turned toward right field to acknowledge the Bleacher Creatures, because they'd been such a big part of my experience in New York—of the four championships, of every inning, and of each strikeout.

A few times, I would take the subway to the game and walk around the area behind the bleachers along River Avenue. It's a unique neighborhood, almost hidden by the ballpark. There was a buzz on those blocks, the sort of aura that makes old urban ballparks feel very different. When I finally retired after a brief stint with the Red Sox, I came back to watch a game in the right-field bleachers. I told everybody I would, and maybe they didn't believe me. But I'd been a player for so long that I had never watched a major league game from the stands. I wanted to do it there, behind the right-field wall, on Opening Day 2002. I wanted to take in that vantage point, to see what the Bleacher Creatures were all about.

Initially, I had to kiss and make up with the Creatures about that little Boston stretch of mine. After I was granted forgiveness, I followed some of the fans around, doing everything they told me to do. And it was great. The Bleacher Creatures were wonderful. They let me kick off the roll call, yell at Bernie Williams, and taunt the box seaters. They showed me the sacred bench that was home to the late great Ali Ramirez, the original cowbell man. I became involved in all the chants and got the sense that I was part of a big social club out there. It was a new experience to watch plays unfold from this angle and distance. We saw the doubles down the line and the long fly balls in the gap. We watched Bernie chase them down. We drove the security guards a little crazy, and I don't think I made Mr. Steinbrenner very happy that day with my little adventure. But it was a lot of fun, and everybody was in great spirits.

They're always in great spirits in the bleachers, full of life and outrage. I'd be happy to share with them any season, any celebration of baseball, or any pages in a book.

—DAVID CONE

David Cone (far right) hangs with Bleacher Creatures Donald Simpson and Milton Ousland during Opening Day 2002. (Larry Palumbo/Coyote Magic Photography)

PREFACE

The first time I went to Yankee Stadium, I didn't sit in the bleachers. It was 1957, I was just five years old, and my father walked with me east from Washington Heights in Manhattan, over the McCombs Dam Bridge and down into the mysterious Bronx.

Baseball is different than the other sports in this way. We place it within the context of family, of place, of occasion, and all five senses are deeply involved in the process. My father was a Czech immigrant with no boyhood connections to baseball. Yet he inherently grasped that this was an important pastime in America. He learned the game and pitched to his son, who had a bad habit of swinging the bat vertically instead of horizontally.

On the stroll to the park that day, I looked down to the left at the Polo Grounds, and my dad explained to me that the New York Giants played in that building (though not for long!). You easily could view two Major League Baseball parks from the same spot at ground level, a sight that will never be experienced again, anywhere, because the economics would be prohibitive. After working our way up the ramps inside Yankee Stadium and claiming our general admission seats miles above home plate, I recall being amazed, as only a city kid could, by the enormous patch of green laid out before me. This wasn't just a ball field, not like any I'd seen before. This was a national park.

I have few memories of that first game, other than the grassy expanse, a wafting, diffused cigar smell that I will always associate with baseball viewing, and one particular play in which Enos Slaughter tagged up at third base and beat a relay to the plate. Many years later I would discover that Slaughter was a mean son of a gun. But at that moment he was a hero in pinstripes, and the Yankees were on their way toward another American League pennant. I bought a Mickey Mantle action figure, which would be worth thousands on the collectibles market today, and I was committed to serious fanhood. My father and I returned often over the next few years to sit in the left-field bleachers, some of the best seats in the house until the stadium was renovated in the mid-1970s. Then those seats were pushed too far back from the playing field, behind the mind-numbing, pretentious Monument Park.

That is the story of one conversion, one path to a pinstriped obsession that I carried inside my gut until sports journalism got the better of me. Once I started rooting for games to finish before the arrival of my newspaper deadline, I could never go home again, emotionally. But there are still millions of true believers, and their pinstriped passions can be traced, through primal ancestral roots, to that moment in time when the stadium was first constructed on a 10-acre lot in the southwest Bronx. The Yankees purchased the land in 1921 for $675,000 from the estate of William Waldorf Astor, a man of considerable wealth and pedigree. The club owner, Colonel Jacob Ruppert, felt boldly empowered by the team's new popularity, after he acquired Babe Ruth from the Boston Red Sox in 1920 for $125,000 plus a $350,000 loan toward the mortgage on Fenway Park. The Yankees had been sharing the Polo Grounds with the Giants, but now the Yanks with Ruth were outdrawing their landlords, and the furious Giants told the Yankees to take a cross-river hike.

The new stadium was an enormous investment, a triple-decked wonder of the world that could seat 74,200 fans. The architects were from Cleveland, coincidentally, although no direct antecedents of the Steinbrenner family. For $2.5 million, White Construction Company completed the place at an impressive pace by today's standards, ready for Opening Day in 1923. Not only was it the House that Ruth Built, it was the House Built for Ruth. The right-field foul pole was merely 295 feet from home plate, and a porch extended out toward center that enabled the mighty Babe to reach the stands without making perfect contact on the ball. There were 16 bathrooms built into the stadium (that's one for every 4,637 customers), a fact that was trumpeted as a major breakthrough in customer convenience. The building opened to a packed house against the Red Sox on April 18, 1923, with hundreds of fans hanging about outside the stadium looking for a ticket. The scene was not unlike today's Opening Days, with 56,000 fans inside and scalpers patrolling the outside for desperate buyers. The Babe blasted a three-run shot that day to beat Boston 4-1. It was a poetic start to an epic tale of success.

When Ruth hit that homer, the ball carried into an area that few people in Section 39 of the bleachers would recognize today. Original plans for the park called for its three decks to encircle the entire park. The Osborne Engineering Company proposed an enclosed building "impenetrable to all human eyes, save those of aviators." This was simply too expensive, however, and temporary wooden stands were installed instead around the outfield. Without a roof directly overhead, fans were "bleached" by the sun, a prerequisite characteristic of all true bleachers.

Close by, a copper façade, an architectural trademark of the stadium, hung down from the roof of the third deck. There was another feature that proved, thankfully, less permanent: The playing field sloped upward throughout what is now the warning track area. That hill was most pronounced in right, where Ruth played his position, where Ruth hit most of his balls, and where the Bleacher Creatures prowl today. There were ads then, too, above the bleachers and a giant scoreboard to post out-of-town scores. And just like today, those early Yankees fans appreciated a championship. Damon Runyan, the colorful New York newspaperman, described what happened at the stadium on October 9, 1927, after the Yankees swept the Pirates in the World Series with a 4-3 victory on a wild pitch from Pittsburgh pitcher John Miljus in the bottom of the ninth inning:

"The crowd from the boxes and the lower stands immediately swept over the field, cheering wildly, and John Miljus, who had almost been a hero, worked his way through the mob, swinging his pitching glove dejectedly over by the Yankee[s] bench. The New York players were fighting their way out of their dugout while the fans reached eager hands for them. The fans seemed particularly anxious to grab the large mitts of Mr. George Herman "Babe"

Ruth, whose second home run of the series, a drive into the right-field bleachers in the fifth, apparently stowed the game away right then and there…"

There were regrettable incidents back then in the crowd, just as there are occasionally today. In 1934, a particularly aggressive stadium security guard fractured the skull of a teenage boy, David Levy, as he attempted to get himself a souvenir by pulling a baseball from the screen behind home plate. The ball had been fouled back by no less a star than Lou Gehrig. Levy eventually won $7,500 in damages from the Yankees, and the nasty affair contributed to a new league-wide policy allowing fans to keep balls whenever they flew into the stands.

By 1937, the grandstands at the stadium were extended beyond the foul pole. The wooden bleachers were replaced by a concrete foundation. The Yankees' outrageous pattern of success had been established and, because of all the winning, the team's fans acquired a reputation for complacency and front-running. At the time, it was not altogether undeserved. From 1932 through 1945, despite enormous success, the Yanks never cracked the million mark in season attendance. In 1943, for example, the Yankees finished first by 13½ games on the way to a World Series victory, yet drew only 645,006 fans, an average of about 9,000 fans per home game. A postwar boom and the return of Joe DiMaggio rejuvenated interest in a big way, boosting attendance to more than two million for five straight seasons, but there was no arguing that the Yankees' crowd at the time was not nearly so passionate as the one supporting the Brooklyn Dodgers. The most dedicated fans in New York, and around the country, were the ones who took great pleasure and grief in rooting against the Yankees.

James Thurber, the novelist, wrote that "the majority of American males put themselves to sleep by striking out the batting order of the New York Yankees." It was either Joe E. Lewis, the comedian, or Jimmy Little, the actor, who first remarked that, "Rooting for the Yankees is like rooting for U.S. Steel." Red Smith, the great columnist, was the first to report that pointed comment in the newspaper. Jimmy Cannon, the most direct of all city columnists, sneered that "rooting for the Yankees is like owning a yacht." And when the Yankees beat the Giants in the 1951 World Series, Cannon wrote in the *New York Post*, "Most of the town pulled for the Giants." Cheering for the Yankees became an act of classism, of chronic snobbery. Yankees supporters were viewed as stuffy, unimaginative aristocrats. The stadium took on the tone and appearance of a mausoleum. The warning-track area in center-sprouted monuments to Ruppert, Ruth, and Gehrig that looked like tombstones right there on the field of play. They only reinforced the notion that the stadium was a museum to wealth and winning, not a place of sporting joy and spontaneous celebration.

It didn't help that the Yanks lagged far behind the Dodgers and Giants when it came to integrating their roster with an African-American star. Elston Howard didn't arrive until 1955, eight years after Jackie Robinson came to Brooklyn. Later, even during the four seasons when New York featured only one major league team, from 1958 through 1961, the Yankees did not necessarily charm the entire city. Many fans waited patiently for the Mets to arrive, refusing to switch allegiances to the hated American Leaguers. On October 1, 1961, when Roger Maris struck his 61st home run to break Babe Ruth's mark, there were only 23,154 fans inside Yankee Stadium to applaud politely as Maris rounded the bases on his way to history, with an asterisk.

Really, it wasn't until George Steinbrenner purchased the team in 1973 and after the stadium was remodeled and reopened in 1976 that the Yankees became a hot ticket again in New York. This edition was an electrifying twist on an old theme: The rich got still richer. The Yanks became pioneers in signing free agents, talented and brimming with ego. The high-powered infighting among the marquee names on this club inspired the swarming media to dub the Yankees clubhouse, The Bronx Zoo. Reggie Jackson, Billy Martin, and Thurman Munson won a couple of championships, but they also changed the image of the team and toughened the fan in the stands. Suddenly, the Yankees and their crowd were a raucous, multicultural bunch, no longer gentlemen Bombers. The

Yanks had become a part of the city's fabric, and that was soon reflected in the demographics of their supporters.

Blacks and Hispanics embraced the team, in part because of African-American, Latin-American, and Caribbean talents such as Reggie, Chris Chambliss, Derek Jeter, Bernie Williams, Mariano Rivera, Orlando "El Duque" Hernandez, and Jorge Posada. The Yanks no longer seemed hopelessly out of place in the Bronx. They were selling out for the bigger games, and the New York fans became known as both smart and intimidating. At times—like when 12-year-old Jeffrey Maier intercepted a fly ball during a play-off game in October 1996, turning it into a homer against the Orioles—the fans seemed capable of directly determining the outcome of important games.

In the bleachers, where the price of a game ticket remained stubbornly stuck in single digits, the democracy was most evident. Here was the greatest bargain in professional sports. While corporate types paid more than $100 per box seat at Knicks, Mets, Rangers, and Yankees games, the Bleacher Creatures enjoyed exquisite camaraderie and a convenient second home at a very reasonable price.

Ever since the 1976 remodeling, the right-field bleachers have become a far better place to watch the game than the left-field bleachers. On the left, there is Monument Park, which stands somberly between the fans and the field. But on the right-field side, there is still nothing in the way. Fans in Sections 37, 39, or 41 can reach out and practically touch players as they shag flies before the game. Fans praise and taunt right fielders, who hear every word. Batting practice baseballs bounce into this region, again and again, making for easy pickings.

The view from Section 39 in the right-field bleachers is unlike any other vista at Yankee Stadium or in the South Bronx. Everything is backward, swiveled 180 degrees—Alice through the looking glass and beyond the warning track. Twitchy fielders are faced flush in the opposite direction, rudely swaying their rumps behind them. Pitchers hurl 90-mile per hour cutters at the plate, 400 feet away from the strained eyeballs of squinting bleacher analysts. Was that a curve? A slider? Batters swing hard, hoping to knock a baseball far and hard into the Section 39 masses, with little or no concern about the scramble that will follow for the souvenir.

Maybe it is impossible to discern a ball from strike out here and to offer a convincing argument on a close call at first. Maybe those flat plastic benches aren't the most comfortable of thrones. Maybe if the guy in front of you stands up at the wrong time, you miss the double into the left-field gap. But on the whole, this is quite a place, inhabited by a unique form of spectator.

The Bleacher Creatures have created their own *Lord of the Flies* political and social order, rolling quite literally around the aisles after home run balls, gulping smuggled alcohol in uncanny volumes, and screaming at box-seat fans, "You paid 30, we paid 8!" Their sight line would be considered alienating, even demoralizing, if it weren't for the sense of community that reaches from atop Row WW, near the Utz Potato Chips sign, down toward Gary Sheffield patrolling right field, to Jason Giambi or Tony Clark at first base, and then straight on into the Yankees dugout. The Bleacher Creatures' sphere of influence is not limited by the deep-blue outfield walls or by the chalk-white foul lines. Regardless of what is going on in their working and personal lives, these fans have become a vibrant part of the pinstriped fabric that defines the relentless Yankees dynasty.

Come for the game, stay for the company. The community matters as much here as the championship banners. Many authors have waxed poetically about the nature of fanhood, about the agonies of rooting for the Boston Red Sox, Chicago Cubs, or Brooklyn Dodgers. But these efforts were mostly intellectual explorations, odes to despair and to loyalty and to the great sport of baseball. I wanted instead to chronicle the actual lives of these fans, to get inside their skins and their daily ordeals, in order to understand their extraordinary commitment. Almost all of them welcomed the intrusion. When I began reporting the book, only one bleachers regular said she wanted no part of it, and a couple of others asked to be identified solely by their Bleacher Creature monikers, not by their outside-world names.

So it was here in Section 39 that I sat gratefully among friends, baked by the sun or illuminated by the mercury lamps, during a 2004 season filled with enormous promise and potential pratfalls. It was nearly half a century since I'd first laid eyes on the Bronx building and the national park inside. And this time, I was sitting in the bleachers.

ACKNOWLEDGMENTS

This book would have been pointless, and impossible, if the Bleacher Creatures hadn't accepted me over the past decade as a worthy chronicler of their escapades. To those mentioned in this book and to those who are not, thanks for the company and the quotes.

It was a former sports editor at the *Daily News*, Barry Werner, who first sent me into the bleachers for a fan story. And it is the current sports editor, Leon Carter, who keeps sending me back.

Thanks also to Mike Pearson, for signing up this labor of love; to Elisa Bock Laird, for editing what there is of it; and to Andrew Levy, who made the foreword with David Cone happen.

Finally, thanks to my dad, for dragging me to a Yankees game when I was probably too young to know what I was watching.

INTRODUCTION

I called Tina Lewis in February, a few days after the Yankees traded for Alex Rodriguez. I was sincerely worried about her health—she had been undergoing treatment for cancer, and besides I wanted to hear her opinion on such a world-inverting transaction.

On the outgoing message of her ever-changing cell phone number, Tina (who preferred this spelling to the more official, Teena) identified herself as the "queen of the bleachers," for good reason. Ever since the original cowbell man, Ali Ramirez, died back in 1996, Tina took over in Section 39 as chief organizer and lobbyist for the disenfranchised Creatures. She assumed Ali's throne, quite literally, after successfully lobbying the Yankees to bolt down a plaque on the plastic bench to commemorate Ali. Every year on the anniversary of his death, Tina laid a bouquet of flowers on what had become her own seat to honor Ali. If you wanted to be recognized as a true Creature, you needed to pass the Tina test. That meant you attended countless Detroit and Cleveland games over several seasons, not just the high-profile Red Sox and Mets showdowns. Only then would she believe in your commitment to pinstripes.

When I first started writing about the Creatures for the *Daily News*, back in September 1996, it didn't take long to figure out who was the leader of the pack. All rows led to Tina and to her booming cheers. When she approved of me, I was accepted as the group's unofficial chronicler. Until then, there were some delicate moments among the Creatures. I remember how Bad Mouth Larry Palumbo, now a friend and the official photographer for this book, once was quite furious at me over the oddest of disagreements. A woman had flashed her breasts to the bleachers from the upper deck, and I quoted Larry in a column as saying, "I've never seen that before." He meant that he'd never seen a woman do that from the upper deck, but Larry thought the article made him sound like somebody who had never seen women's breasts. I ran a funny correction of sorts, with careful phrasing that befitted a family newspaper. Larry wasn't entirely satisfied.

"Bondy's the kind of guy, if he wasn't writing about us, we'd be beating him up!" Larry said.

He didn't mean it, of course, and even if he did, Tina wouldn't have let it happen.

There were many Creature-imposed rules in the right-field bleachers at Yankee Stadium that had nothing to with the stuff you read in the small print on the back of a ticket stub, and Tina enforced them all. The Yankees did not allow cursing or alcohol or standing on the benches in the bleachers. The Creatures strived to break many of those laws but had their own more proletarian codes. They had their own secret handshake, a triple high-five that was reluctantly utilized by all ("That's three more times than I really want to touch anybody," Larry groused). They did not allow dress ties in the bleachers. Ties were a symbol of the workplace, and the bleachers had nothing to do with work. If you wore one, you were harassed until you removed it. There was to be no giant beachball bouncing in the bleachers. No face painting. No dancing of the Macarena, or any such gimmicky fad. The Wave was most definitely prohibited, viewed as a symptom of attention deficit disorder for spectators. It was considered far too frivolous in such a serious rooting environment. No cell phones were allowed, except for emergencies. Only one cowbell was permitted, franchised to Milton Ousland at the moment, although he was pushing his luck. The presence of high school bands, on the sacred field where Ruth and Mantle once galloped, was frowned upon. And, most of all, nobody was permitted to wear a cap or jersey, or carry a banner, that supported another team—at risk of losing the offensive item by force. During heated moments, Mets and Red Sox caps, in particular, were known to go up in flames, as if by magic (though never while on anybody's head!).

One of the Creatures' most admirable traits was their indifference toward fiscal and material stature. A member of the tribe was not judged by the size of his or her wallet. If a fan received a promotion or a raise, it mattered little to the fans in Section 39. Though there was plenty of political and romantic back-biting, there was no petty jealousy in regard to money. Everybody wished everyone else the wherewithal to make it through another 24 hours, until the next game. Financial and vocational dealings from that other life, outside Section 39, had no real impact on the nine innings of Yankees baseball. When Donald Simpson became an instant millionaire after receiving compensation from a special 9/11 victims fund, he was treated no differently than when he was struggling to make ends meet. Simpson would have had it no other way. The majority of the regular bleachers fans were male, in their 20s, and just starting to make their way through life. But this was a multiethnic, diverse bunch from all over the New York–New Jersey–Connecticut region. The bleachers fans were willing to accept into their midst resilient women (better make that *very* resilient women), the young (with progressive parents), and the elderly (preferably hard of hearing), regardless of income levels.

In 2000, the Yankees started selling bleachers seats as season ticket packages, and suddenly each Creature had to dredge up a minimum of $368 to fund his or her increasingly expensive habit. Individual seats still cost a relatively modest $8 as part of the package, but fans were being asked for a 46-game commitment in order to reserve their spot in Section 39 and to guarantee access to precious playoff tickets. Tina had lived in Queens and New Jersey, wherever she could pay the bills and still find a way to buy or borrow Yankees tickets. Somehow, Tina always came up with the connections. She was the most loyal and faithful of all the Creatures. Once a Yankee won her heart, she did not forsake him if he was traded or benched. She even forgave bleachers favorite David Cone, who fled the Bronx for Boston, of all places, via free agency.

And now, as winter's final snowstorms were drifting to the Northeast and as the southern migration of pitchers and catchers had begun toward Florida, Tina proclaimed herself healthy and had moved back to New York. She'd endured 40 radiation treatments altogether.

"I'm fine, there's no cancer, but my energy level isn't there yet," she said.

Mostly, she was not at all pleased with the A-Rod deal.

"Maybe I'm the only Yankees fan who isn't happy," Tina said. "But I hate Rodriguez. I love Alfonso Soriano. He has always been one of my favorites. I don't like this at all."

Typical Tina. She had become attached to Soriano, and soon enough I was sure she would become attached to Rodriguez. It would take time, though, as it should.

Tina wasn't the only one who lived and died with the comings and goings. The fans felt particularly close to the Yankees players, in part because there was some real interplay during the season. Players would stop to chat outside the press gate before the games, and they would toss balls to Section 39ers during batting practice. Cone, one of the more accessible stars, had visited the bleachers and actually sat there for a game next to his fans. David Wells had promised to do the same once he retired, although you never knew with "Boomer." But baseball was unpredictable with its sad retirements and trades. Gone were such recent heroes as Tino Martinez, Scott Brosius, and the most popular Yankee of all, Paul O'Neill. O'Neill had stood in right field, just in front of Section 39, for nine wonderful years. The Creatures came to know his every ritual, his stretching and his preening. He would throw his shoulders back and whirl his arms backward over his head. O'Neill tipped the bill of his cap. He walked around impatiently and flexed his left knee. He pounded his mitt.

"To tell you the truth," Tina said, "it's been hard. I really miss Pauly. There's nobody out there to cheer for. They keep changing right-fielders every day."

That was just one of the intriguing aspects of 2004. After two seasons of platooning and experimenting in right, the Yankees had signed superstar Gary Sheffield as a free agent. Despite a sore thumb and persistent steroid rumors, Sheffield figured to man the post in front of Section 39 with far more prowess on offense and defense than any of the imposters since O'Neill. Sheffield batted .330 with 39 homers in 2003. He had a decent arm, too, when it was on target. The Creatures, eager for a steady and sturdy presence in right, were thrilled about this addition. Even Tina.

There were other transactions, too, inspired by George Steinbrenner to remain a step ahead of the Boston Red Sox. As yet, it was unclear which of the archrivals had enjoyed the better off season. The Red Sox filled two gaping holes. They signed free agent Curt Schilling to be their co-ace with Pedro Martinez. Boston also plugged its most glaring weakness in the bullpen by acquiring former Oakland stopper Keith Foulke, who had a 2.08 ERA and 43 saves in 2003. Other than that, the Red Sox stood pat, which meant they stood with plenty. Their offense had been spectacular in 2003, the best in the league. The Sox figured to be no worse in 2004, probably better, as they resumed their obsessive chase and reignited the inferiority complex sprung from the famous Ruthian transaction in 1920.

The Yanks had been significantly remodeled during the off season. Andy Pettitte, the most reliable of starters, and Roger Clemens left for Houston, both citing homesickness. Wells, the Creatures' favorite, went to San Diego to be closer to his own home. That defection hurt badly, because this was the second time that Wells escaped the Bronx during his career, and he was truly a kindred Creature spirit. Among his many attributes, the rotund Wells owned a fighting spirit, as evidenced by his late-night brawl in a city diner. Such shenanigans cemented his place forever among the immortals, as far as the bleachers fans were concerned. Now Wells was gone, along with the straight-arrow Pettitte and the manic mercenary, Clemens. In their stead were a couple of extremely talented starters—Javier Vazquez, acquired from the eternally bankrupt Expos, and Kevin Brown, the fragile and surly former Dodger. The middle relief had been significantly upgraded. The manager, Joe Torre, was hinting that he might be willing to extend his own contract beyond the end of the season, after all. Taken as a whole, things were uncertain, but promising.

The Creatures had been spoiled rotten during the Bombers' run from 1996 to 2000, when the Yankees captured four titles in five years. The same fans learned recently, painfully, that even the

$180 million-plus Yankees payroll provided no guarantees. Fans of other less successful teams harrumphed at the suggestion that Yankees fans, with their 39 American League championships, were acquainted with suffering. But baseball was a religion in New York, and the Creatures were fundamentalists. When the 2003 World Series against Florida unraveled, beginning with Game 4, there was real heartache. Three years without a 27th World Championship was a lengthy drought, by Yankees standards, and a remedy was in order. The Creatures truly believed they could influence the outcome of games, and therefore they accepted some responsibility for the team's recent spate of disappointing endings.

It was with this zealous pinstriped resolve that bleachers fans approached the new season, another opportunity to add a banner and to humiliate the Mets, the Red Sox, the Wall Streeters, the face painters, the box seaters. The box seats were separated from the bleachers by a concrete rampway about 10 yards wide, but of course the rift was far greater than that. The Creatures felt they were the only true believers. The partition was more about mind-set than about distance. There were 5,309 seats in the bleachers—3,054 of them in left and 2,255 in right. Each section in the right-field bleachers represented a different manifestation of this commitment. Section 37, closest to the right-field foul pole, was filled with young blood, with the upstarts. Section 39 was the old guard, the keepers of the flame and guardians of the rituals. Section 41 was the spillover, the holding pen. There were maybe 300 core Creatures out here altogether, spread out over an area of benches that encompassed about 1,000 seats. This was the prime real estate. Anyplace else, especially the left-field bleachers, was Siberia.

The winter had been particularly long and stubborn, with snowstorms ambushing the area from late November to mid-March. The Yankees opened their regular season against Tampa Bay in Japan, a surreal journey to the Far East in late March. They would return for the sold-out home opener April 8, and the fans in Section 39 would be there in force. Tina said she'd meet us that afternoon, on the roof of the parking garage across the street from the stadium. There would be the usual barbecue.

CAST OF CHARACTERS
(IN ORDER OF APPEARANCE)

TINA LEWIS—Queen of the bleachers, the caretaker of Section 39. Before reserved seats came into play, Tina would block off and defend the benches for the core Creatures.

ALI RAMIREZ—The original cowbell man, revered as one of the founding fathers. When he died in 1996, a commemorative plaque was screwed onto his bench seat.

BAD MOUTH LARRY—Larry Palumbo has one of the dirtiest, funniest mouths in the bleachers. He is the official photographer of this book.

MILTON, THE COWBELL MAN—Milton Ousland took over cowbell duties from Ali, although he is constantly taking heat from fellow Creatures for his spotty attendance record.

DONALD SIMPSON—The bleachers' only known millionaire. Big D suffered a back injury and trauma during 9/11 when he was working for a phone company at the World Trade Center.

BLUE LOU—Organizer and chef extraordinaire of barbecues before Opening Day and big playoff games. Leader of the ornery splinter group, The Squid, which opposes all media coverage.

BALD VINNY—Chief cheerleader and instigator of the famous first-inning roll call. His T-shirt stand on River Avenue outside the bleachers entrance has become a hangout spot and meeting place.

BALD RAY—One of the Section 39 regulars, a young grandfather, a U.N. worker, and genuinely upbeat guy.

MIKE DONAHUE—A garrulous Creature and bartender at a college tavern in New Rochelle, New York. Famous for smuggling alcohol into the bleachers in imaginative fashions.

KNOBLAUCH—Mike March was nicknamed "Knoblauch" because this mailman looks a lot like the former Yankees second baseman. He owns an incredible assortment of Yankees pins.

MIDGET MIKE—Mike Milianta, a mailman and longtime Section 39 regular, somehow went from "Little Mike" to "Midget Mike" over the years. He voices the most negative attitude in the bleachers on a daily basis, but he's just a softie at heart.

JESSICA HEROLD—A Rutgers student and bleachers regular who has put up with far too much teasing from the Creatures over her earnest studies.

PAUL KAPLAN—Before he lost a lot of weight and semi-retired from rooting, Kaplan would entertain the Creatures with his painful roll along the benches during the seventh-inning stretch.

NATURE BOY—The Ric Flair impersonator from Section 37 who regularly annoys the Creatures from Section 39 with his non-sequitur chants of "Whoo!"

JON ZERON—A bleachers traditionalist who is annoyed by any changes at Yankee Stadium, particularly the new organist.

TONE CAPONE—A particularly naughty and insightful Creature who may have been thrown out of more games than any other fan.

LUIGI—Luis Castillo was a teenaged Creature from Section 39 when he was hired as a batboy and then as a clubhouse worker by the Yankees. He was nicknamed "Luigi" by David Cone and the Yankees players. "Luigi" was beaten to within an inch of his life in a South Bronx street incident but survived and continues to work tirelessly in the Yankees clubhouse.

SHERIFF TOM BROWN—For nearly a decade, (not really a) sheriff, Tom was the inspirational leader of the Creatures, full of mischief and wisecracks. Known to deputize many women in the bleachers. More recently, he has settled into the role of father and husband but occasionally makes cameo appearances.

TOM, THE UNDERCOVER COP—Snarling Mets fan who takes great pleasure in his role as villain when he tickets or hassles Creatures for drinking or other trespasses.

G.B. STEVE—A core Creature from Staten Island and one of the key softball game organizers.

MR. MANGO—An alternative pregame barbecue host to Blue Lou.

UPTOWN MIKE—A good friend to Donald Simpson and Diggity Dan. Uptown Mike is known to come on every giveaway promotion and has a collection of every free Yankees gift.

GROVER—Self-proclaimed greatest comedian of all time. He will criticize others' jokes whenever possible.

WALKMAN JOHN—A fanatic scorecard keeper who landed the perfect job: working as a statistician for the Elias Sports Bureau.

MSB—Marc Chalpin uses an unprintable pseudonym attacking the Mets, hence the three initials. Chalpin can get under the skin of some fellow Creatures but gets big points for his commitment.

KWIK—Organizes trips to Toronto games, like the one that was halted briefly by the Creatures' misbehavior.

ANTHONY BALOO—Moderator of the fans' website, www.section39.com. He has a tendency to react emotionally to wins or losses, posting doomsday messages on the site.

DIGGITY DAN—Also known as Mr. Box Seat, because he will occasionally abandon the bleachers for the box seats.

EVELYN—A friend who helped Tina through some of her toughest times.

CUBAN MONICA—A Section 37 regular who tries very hard to keep her liberal political bent to herself, thereby avoiding many arguments.

NORMA—One of the Section 37 originals and one of the few 37ers dearly respected by Section 39. Very shy. She hates to be quoted.

IRIS—Iris is Norma's occasional nemesis, another longtime Section 37 denizen who sits nearby. The two middle-aged women get into very amusing arguments.

TERENCE WILLIAMS—Head of Yankee Stadium security detail in the bleachers. Terence is a Mets fan, but the Creatures generally get along with him. If necessary, however, he will kick out a fan or two.

STATMAN—Steve Tipa from Section 37 (by way of Flushing) wears thick glasses and is the final authority on all scorecard and statistical issues involving the Yankees.

SONIA—Another of Tina's friends, a quipster.

ROSE—Patient, saintly girlfriend of Bald Vinny. Rose met Vinny in the bleachers, and by the end of the season the couple was getting ready to move together into an Astoria, Queens, apartment.

CHRIS CARTELLI—A popular Creature who quit the bleachers after several seasons and was last seen in the stands behind home plate somewhere.

X-PAC—Another Creature nicknamed after a pro wrestler. Also known as Jesus because of his long hair.

JUNIOR—Regularly raises the Panamanian flag in Section 39 and tells people to stand up every inning for every potential rally even if the Yankees are losing 9-0.

PHIL—Mr. Make It Happen is always in the middle of things, including the brawl at the softball game with Bad Mouth Larry.

THE DEVER—Member of The Squid. A big soccer fan, and someone who takes occasional exception to the antics of Nature Boy in Section 37.

"41"— The greatest Kiss fan of all time, from Section 41.

ISRAELI JOE—Reformed alcoholic and one of the Section 37 regulars. Says he's not Jewish but spent some time in Israel.

CONNECTICUT JOE—One of the leaders of Section 37, a hefty guy with a sweet personality.

POLIZZOTTIS—The family sits in Section 37 sometimes and unofficially adopted Israeli Joe.

STONE COLD—Yet another pro wrestler imitator. He looks remarkably like his namesake and leads fans in chants that promise to "open a can of whup ass" on opponents.

OLD MAN SAM—Not really old at all, but his new friends in Section 37 (Sam is a defector from 39) like to refer to him that way because of his seniority.

OLD MAN JIMMY—Unlike Sam, Jimmy is old. Just don't tell him. He remains one of the most active and devoted of the Creatures.

EMERSON—A young nine-year-old fan in Section 37 being touted as the next great spectator by those who have scouted him.

BIG KEN—Another proud Section 37 booster.

LITTLE ROB—Nothing little about him. Rob, from Section 37, says he's had enough of Milton Ousland's cowbell playing.

CHRIS HIGGINS—A particularly jovial Section 39 regular and nephew of bestselling author Mary Higgins Clark.

FACE—He throws himself on the floor and gets dirty after homers.

SUZY—A distant cousin of Tina's and a bleachers regular, who has dated several of the Creatures. A burgeoning sportswriter, Suzy is knowledgeable about her baseball and has one of the longest shelf lives among women in Section 39.

FOURDOGG4LIFE—Screen name of a www.section39.com member, who defends the honor of Section 41, attacking both Sections 39 and 37.

DAN MOFSENSON—A regular who had the nerve to sell a playoff ticket to Midget Mike at a marginal profit.

MTA JOE—An employee of the Metropolitan Transit Authority and one of the most visible and reliable Creatures.

TONE 516—A young up-and-comer, winner of Rookie of the Year two seasons ago. Longtimers say he provides the spunk and edge that was blunted by too many championships.

MILES—A sportswriter with *The Village Voice* and well-reasoned world observer.

SANDY—A personable Creature who feuded briefly with Tina.

BALD TEDDY—Teddy was a particularly boisterous Section 39er during the championships seasons. He left to teach in Kansas.

CHICO—The unofficial bookie of the bleachers.

JODIE FOSTER—A former regular who resembled, somewhat, the actress Jodie Foster. She left for a career.

ROB ANDRADE—Another former regular infamous for juggling women and shamelessly boasting about it.

VANESSA—An ex-Creature viewed very nostalgically. Or, as Donahue puts it, a hottie.

```
APRIL 8, 2004                    SEASON RECORD (3-2)

                 123  456  789    R  H  E
WHITE SOX        000  100  000    1  4  1
YANKEES          200  001  00X    3  7  1
```

HOME
OPENER

Opening Day 2004 arrived in all its urban glory, on a welcome and unseasonably mild day. The South Bronx was made over again, from the bustle inside the bodegas to the milling crowds on River Avenue, busy browsing the goods at Stan's Baseball Land. Stan's was a multitentacled, blocklong Yankees bazaar and saloon along the backside of the stadium by the bleachers' entrance. No merchandise was off limits. Stan's had recently expanded into pinstriped ladies' lingerie. On the opposite side of the stadium, outside home plate, a fire-engine red calliope played, "Take Me Out to the Ball Game," in a pleasant, fluty voice that carried for blocks. On early April days here, there was little of the edginess and aggressive policing that drained the fun and mischief from October playoff nights. Fans were lined up at the box office windows, smiling, hoping somehow to land tickets for a game that had been sold out for months. Most of these customers would later turn to scalpers in desperation, as the first pitch approached. And on the roof of the parking garage, across the street from the stadium, alongside the elevated subway line where the No. 4 train rumbled past, the Bleacher Creatures began to gather for their great feast.

Word of Blue Lou's barbecue had spread to those in the know through the Bleacher Creatures website, www.section39.com, and by word of cell phone. It was quite the banquet. There were ribs, steaks, hot dogs, even grilled vegetables for a balanced pregame meal. A couple of kegs materialized from the back of an SUV. The same cops who'd issued countless summonses for public drinking during the World Series were turning their backs today. The golden liquid flowed from every imaginable container: bottle, can, keg, and thermos.

There were some fences to be mended and some delicate moments ahead. My chronicling of the Creatures had managed to

Blue Lou's legendary barbecue is the place for Section 39ers to gather and reconnect before the game. (Larry Palumbo/Coyote Magic Photography)

offend at least a handful of the Section 39ers. Blue Lou was one of them. He was annoyed that one column had depicted him heroically pitted against the police during the previous autumn and that these patrolmen had hunted down Blue Lou and served him with a $25 ticket for drinking. Another column did him no favors with the women among the Bleacher Creatures. It quoted him calling these female fans, "rugged drunks." In response to such journalistic slights, Blue Lou had recently formed a splinter group, The Squid, which held as its core policy the banishment of meddlesome media types like myself. The group got its name from an animal that squirts ink, much like dreaded sportswriters. But Blue Lou was not mean spirited, and after some negotiating he agreed to place me on probation. If I would deliver a framed apology, he would lift the sentence entirely—but he would not forget about the terms. I needed to deliver the apology.

"You can't hustle a hustler," he warned. Blue Lou was large and formidable.

It was good to see everyone, or nearly everyone, up on that roof. Tina was missing. She wasn't feeling strong enough to come to such a high-profile game. But there was a familiar cast of 30 or so, including most of the regulars: Donald Simpson, the millionaire; Bald Vinny, the eternal entrepreneur, who already had a new line of T-shirts ready for sale, with the logo: "Embrace the Hate"; Bald Ray, who brought a Yankees flag that had been signed by the 82nd Airborne in Iraq, where his nephew served; Mike Donahue, who was showing off photos of himself and the beautiful woman bartenders at the New Rochelle bar where he worked; Mike March, also known as Knoblauch, because of his resemblance to the ex-Yankees second baseman; Milton Ousland, the cowbell man; Midget Mike, who was being even more negative than usual; and Jessica Herold (who preferred the name Nymphie), a Rutgers student who was writing her thesis on swelling breasts. She made a futile attempt to discuss her studies seriously and in some detail, while being derided by her fellow Creatures.

"I'm trying to have an adult discussion here," she kept saying.

It wasn't going to work.

There was some talk about the road trip planned by the fans for June, this time to Los Angeles for an interleague series against the Dodgers. These trips were always the source of great misadventures and storytelling. But that was still two months off. For now, baseball issues involving the Yankees were dissected, with some anxiety. On paper, even without the ailing Kenny Lofton, the starting lineup for this home opener was other-worldly: Derek Jeter at short, Bernie Williams in center, Alex Rodriguez at third, Jason Giambi at first, Gary Sheffield in right, Jorge Posada at catcher, Hideki Matsui in left, Ruben Sierra at designated hitter, and Enrique Wilson at second. The Bombers already had completed a tour of Japan and then zipped down to Tampa Bay for two more games. They owned a 2-2 record that didn't reveal much of anything. Mike Mussina had been awful, twice, but then he always needed to fall into a routine. The trip to Japan was jarring for him. The Creatures were correctly more concerned with the No. 4 and No. 5 starter spots.

"Don't worry," Milton, the cowbell man, said. "By the All-Star break, the Yankees will have Randy Johnson."

Milton displayed his cowbell, to show everyone that it was in fact the same bashed-in, rusty model that led the team to the World Series in 2003.

"I've got to spend my money on other things," Milton said.

When Ali Ramirez died in 1996, there was a bit of a political struggle over the question of his cowbell successor. One of Ramirez's young relatives seemed a natural, but he didn't come to enough games. Milton was willing to show up for most of them.

"I didn't really have a choice," said Tina Lewis, who more or less made the final determination on Milton's behalf.

The Creatures teased him about his musical ability ("He's the only Spanish person without rhythm," said Paul Kaplan, a long-time Creature), but Milton was a true professional. He took his lumps. There was that time in the playoffs when Milton fell off a curb at Times Square, sprained his ankle, and required an ambulance to bring him home. But other than that, he generally showed up on time for the biggest games.

Milton was always there for the openers. He had to be, because strange things happened at these events, like the one in 2002. Back then, the Creatures were barbecuing on the roof before the game, and someone mentioned that former Yankees and Mets pitcher David Cone might drop in on the bleachers. He had promised as much, on a radio show.

"If he doesn't bring the beer, he's out," Mike Donahue decided.

Nobody believed he would really come. But then Cone showed, just as he said he would, sporting a brown leather jacket and smiling wide under his golf cap. He wasn't wearing a tie, he didn't paint his face and he wasn't knocking around a beachball. So the Creatures let him stay. It was shocking to see a big league pitcher hanging out with the commoners. Before he was officially welcomed, however, there was a question that needed answering.

"How come you played for the Red Sox last year?" Bald Vinny demanded.

"It's going to take all day to give that answer," Cone said.

He sounded apologetic enough. Plus he was unemployed. So he was forgiven for that unfortunate episode in Boston and those nightmarish Mets seasons. Try as they might to be cool, the Creatures had fallen all over themselves, chatting up and hanging out with their new pal, who was given the nickname Big League David.

"Who was the last Yankee to sit with you people?" they screamed at the box seaters.

And, of course, the box seaters had no answer.

So that was 2002, a classic opener, and there were other tales to tell, too, at the 2004 barbecue. Much meat was chewed, much beer was gulped. Fans showed off their new attire and received extra points for custom-made replica jerseys of extremely obscure ex-Yankees. Danny Tartabull's old shirt (1992-1995) was a good one, but Kevin Maas's No. 23 (1990-1993) was the clear winner. Maas was once supposed to be the next Mickey Mantle but turned into the next Roger Repoz. There was some laughing over this. And then, slowly, the Creatures made their way down the stairs, up the ramp to Section 39, to drink in the atmosphere of the ballpark and to resume old friendships and older grudges. Nature Boy in Section 37, a guy who mimicked the wrestler Ric Flair on every occasion, called all in Section 39 "riff-raff." Little stuff like that drove the Creatures crazy, like the way the Yankees seemed to change everything—except for the alcohol ban in the bleachers—around the stadium each April.

The Creatures hated it when the club rearranged their living space, even if it was just replacing the Kodak sign on the left-field wall with a Canon sign or adding a strikeout counter and some newfangled, psychedelic auxiliary scoreboards along the left- and right-field mezzanines. On the recent trip to Japan, fans were horrified to see that the Yankees sold space on their uniform and their batting helmets to the company Ricoh. Now it looked as if there weren't an inch of space left at the stadium without some form of advertising. The electronic rolling ads so common courtside at basketball arenas had spread, from the wall behind the plate to the walls behind first and third base. And there were other annoyances, like the retirement of an old favorite, organist Eddie Layton.

"The new organist is terrible," Jon Zeron complained. "They should just play old tapes of Eddie."

As usual, Midget Mike was the grumpiest. When the Creatures cheered the introduction of Don Mattingly, "Donny Baseball," the team's new batting coach, Midget Mike stood with thumbs down and booed. Midget Mike was just perpetually cynical. It took a while to get beneath the veneer and realize he was fairly sweet. Feuds, as always, were breaking out everywhere. Midget Mike was angry with Tina Lewis and Tone Capone. Bad Mouth Larry was at war with The Squid, on principle.

Somehow, these disparate rooting factions in the right-field bleachers put aside their differences for three hours as the season was reborn. Bob Sheppard, "The Voice of Yankee Stadium," began his introductions of the 2004 Yankees. George Steinbrenner was busy granting interviews to reporters from the box seats before the game and was reduced to tears when the bleachers fans in left field chanted, "Thank you, George," for buying them another All-Star roster.

Fifteen of the 25 players were new since the 2003 Opening Day. As they trotted out to the first-base line to receive their ovations, it was all too clear these Yankees players were a bit of a mystery. They were extremely talented and expensive, of course. But questions about chemistry, about the defense, and about the starting rotation would not be answered easily. For a sure thing, the Yankees didn't look all that sure footed. Jason Giambi's knees were a mess at first base. Bernie Williams was slowing down in center. Alex Rodriguez was playing out of position at third. There was nobody to play second. After Mussina, Kevin Brown, and Javier Vazquez, the rotation amounted to a lot of wishful thinking. The

Bald Vinny starts off the night with the traditional bleachers roll call. (Larry Palumbo/Coyote Magic Photography)

most optimistic among the fans reassured themselves with this consideration: The Yankees were flawed, but other teams—with the possible exception of the Boston Red Sox—were far less sound.

After a wait of five months, the Yankees, the most experienced and most expensive team in the major leagues, took the field. "The Star-Spangled Banner" was performed, as a group of servicemen carefully unfolded, then folded again, a giant American flag. For the first of what was certain to be many times this season, the Bleacher Creatures chanted for a fan to jump from the upper deck as a human sacrifice to the baseball gods. The guy wouldn't leap. They never did. Steinbrenner, heavy again on the pomp and militarism, staged another Air Force flyover. The jets were a half-minute late but roared overhead after an awkward waiting period. Phil Rizzuto, Yogi Berra, and Whitey Ford threw the ceremonial first pitches, simultaneously. And soon, Vazquez delivered a fastball to start the season in the Bronx.

It was now time for the sacrosanct roll call. This ritual had become the Bleacher Creatures' signature cheer, proof positive that they were very much a part of every ball game. During the 1998 season, at the start of a three-year championship run, the Creatures had instituted this unique first-inning roll call, cited by everyone as a breakthrough in spectator involvement. The players participated in the ritual, making this one of the very few interactive cheers in the history of professional sports. There were also several twists to the roll call. Only a couple of starting pitchers, Cone and Wells, were willing to participate. The Yankees announcers, such as Michael Kay or John Sterling, were sometimes added on for good measure. And as the roll call neared completion, the chant veered in a decidedly more negative direction. Rhythmic heckles were aimed at the Mets, Red Sox, and the opposing right fielder.

This year there was a bit of concern that the newest Yankees starters would not acknowledge the chanting of their names. Bald Vinny started the roll call with the center fielder, as always.

"BURN-Nee... BURN-Nee."

Williams knowingly turned and tipped his glove. Gary Sheffield was next in right.

"Sheff... Sheff... Sheff."

Sheffield not only spun around to acknowledge the Creatures, he tapped his fist to his chest to show his appreciation. The chants continued, along with the top of the first inning.

"MAT-Su-EE...," "EN-REE-KAY...," and, finally, "A-ROD."

Rodriguez was the least comfortable with this procedure and offered only a token tip of the cap. He looked nervous out there and would play that way.

The game itself was reassuring. Vazquez was brilliant from the start, never in real trouble. He pitched three-hit ball for eight innings, and then Mariano Rivera closed out the win. It started to rain during the later innings, yet the Creatures remained until the very end. There was no roof over the bleachers, but the fans there prided themselves on their staying power. Box-seat fans were mocked not only for their expensive tickets (the bleachers were still $8 per seat as part of the season package and $10 on day of game), but also for their tendency to leave the stadium and head for the Major Deegan Expressway at the earliest possible moment.

The Creatures didn't budge. Section 39 was their home, and it was finally open for business again.

"After this one, only 80 home games left," Mike Donahue fretted.

```
               1 2 3   4 5 6   7 8 9      R   H   E
WHITE SOX      0 0 0   0 4 5   0 0 0      9   10  0
YANKEES        0 1 0   0 0 0   0 0 2      3   6   1
```

THE
SECOND
TIME
AROUND

he second home game of the season is never anything like the first. A sense of anticlimax is inevitable, and the raw weather means it's still too early to take these results seriously. Before the second game, Bald Ray was virtually alone on the parking garage roof that afternoon across from the stadium. Blue Lou's barbecue was a distant memory, a smudge of leftover ketchup on the concrete floor.

"Where is everybody?" Ray asked. "They said they were coming."

The Creatures would arrive in due time, for the unusual 4 p.m. start. This was a Friday, and many of them were working.

The bleachers fans often took umbrage at their image as unemployed, raucous drunks. Many didn't mind the raucous drunks reference, but almost all resented the notion that they somehow couldn't hold down a job. Baseball players, managers, and the media were often guilty of sneering at the very fans who supported their game, particularly those spectators who found ways to attend weekday afternoon games. One of the most famous rants in all of baseball was performed by Cubs manager Lee Elia, shortly before his dismissal in 1983, when he characterized the fans at Wrigley Field, his own supporters, as "unemployed." He also labeled them with other more colorful terms that cannot easily be published.

The Creatures in Section 39 were nearly all employed, overemployed, or underemployed in one form or another. Otherwise, they wouldn't have been able to afford those season-ticket packages. Mike March, a.k.a. Knoblauch, was a mailman in Manhattan, with a sore knee that needed repairing again. He was limping along on his route during the late winter when he ran into Alex Rodriguez and entourage, looking for an apartment. Bad Mouth Larry worked in a photo studio. Tone Capone had man-

Luis Castillo, a.k.a. "Luigi," is living the ultimate Bleacher Creature dream—as a clubhouse attendant serving the Yankees he used to cheer for. (Linda Cataffo/New York Daily News L.P.)

aged to hook on with a TV network. Capone always had been one of the wilder bleachers fans, a witty, front-line combatant quite often ejected from games. He also feuded with Midget Mike at length. But as Capone cobbled together a legitimate career, he toned down his act considerably and seemed a bit self-conscious about his past bleachers exploits.

Then there was the ultimate job, surely the most coveted of any landed by a true bleachers denizen. Luis Castillo was a long-time Creature from the South Bronx turned Yankees batboy and clubhouse attendant. He grew up and lived only a 10-minute walk from the stadium. And now, whenever the Yankees won another pennant or World Series, Luis was there to pop open the first bottle of Tattinger's champagne and hand it to Derek Jeter for mischievous spraying purposes.

Luis's job description had changed, slightly. In addition to other duties, he was now in charge of the players' laundry, their dirty pinstripes, hardly a glamorous chore. But he was pleased with the reassignment. The previous year, he had become something of an errand boy to the stars. Luis was bilingual, and he was being ordered about in two languages by some very spoiled baseball players. It got to the point one day when Luis confessed that he would rather be sitting in the bleachers again, as in the good old days, than laboring here inside the Emerald City.

Luis was known as "Luigi" to the Creatures who once sponsored him, and as Squeegee to most of the Yankees players. He had endured harsh times almost beyond description outside the ballpark, particularly after the Yankees beat the Braves for their 25th championship in 1999. He never had much chance that off season to celebrate the team's World Series victory. Two weeks after the Atlanta sweep, Luis, then an 18-year-old senior from the South Bronx attending Wings Academy, was on a college tour in Albany with his school when he received a call from his mother, Milagros Reyes, to come home. His father, Luis Castillo Sr., who suffered with colon cancer for two years, had committed suicide.

The boy was crushed. But youth is resilient, and by the late winter of 1999 Luis was looking greatly forward to the Yankees' return from spring training. Luis had worked as a batboy for the three previous seasons, since writing a letter to a club official at the urging of Tina Lewis. He had befriended several Yanks, most especially David Cone, who taught him how to throw sharper curveballs and cut fastballs. He played baseball in school and kept his grades up, while working extraordinary weeknight hours.

On March 3, 2000, however, his world was again capsized. According to Luis, and to criminal court charges, a stranger assaulted him over a seemingly incidental misunderstanding. Luis and two buddies were heading to a house on Longwood Avenue to watch a boxing match when, Luis said, he accidentally bumped into a woman on the street. Luis exchanged words with the woman.

"She took it the wrong way," he said.

For reasons too frightening to contemplate, her male friend, Wilfredo Rojo-Roca, allegedly took out a gun, aimed at Luis, and pulled the trigger. The gun jammed. Luis ran for his life. He fell. The 42-year-old man then tried to shoot him again. Again, miraculously, the gun jammed. At this point, the man pistol-whipped Luis until the teenager suffered a depressed skull fracture and lost consciousness. Luis spent a week in Lincoln Hospital, where a metal plate was permanently placed in his skull for protection. Luis made it back in time for the 2000 opener. (Rojo-Roca, who had three prior convictions for assault and narcotics, later pleaded guilty to first-degree attempted assault.)

During his first three years with the Yanks, Luis had worked the right-field line during the game as a ball retriever. But he was no longer allowed on the field without medical clearance. He couldn't greet the Bleacher Creatures the way he wanted.

"I love them," he said then. "That's the family that brought me here."

Today, Luis was healthy and running around, even delegating some duties to clubhouse workers with lesser seniority. He had been in touch with Tina Lewis and was concerned for her health. He told me to say hello to the Creatures, and then off he scurried. Gary Sheffield was pulling on a uniform in one corner, away from the media crowded around Jeter. I asked the new Yankee how he enjoyed his first start in right field. He had loved it. Paul O'Neill took him aside during spring training in Florida and gave him some important pointers about the angles and about the fans.

"Paul told me not to be afraid to express myself," Sheffield said. "He said the more I do that, the more the fans will appreciate me."

That was why Sheffield had pounded his chest with his fist and why he had carried on a dialogue with some of the Creatures while the home opener was progressing. It worked like a charm. A-Rod was struggling, still out of place in every way. But Sheffield appeared comfortable in the Bronx, like he was born for the place. The fans out there loved him. They were chanting, "Shef... Shef..." straight through nine innings. Sheffield was pleased with his treatment, as he was with Joe Torre's new three-year $19.2 million contract extension.

"That's as long as I'm going to be here," Sheffield said. "Now I don't have to worry."

All this was very nice, but the second home game did not go well at all. The Creatures' fears about the bottom end of the starting rotation were proven justified, as Jose Contreras lost control of his fastball and was ripped for five runs in five and a third innings. The only nice moment arrived when Bubba Crosby, a hustling fireplug, knocked his first big league homer and practically sprinted around the bases. He became an instant favorite, if only because his name was custom-designed for chanting: "Bub-ba." The Creatures could easily fall in love with this 27-year-old center fielder, still a rookie in terms of major league service. It would be nice if he stuck on the roster, though unlikely. Bubba was infinitely more amiable than Kenny Lofton.

The right-field bleachers were filled to the brim again, but the regulars were noticeably missing. This game was not part of their half-season ticket packages, and some had to work. Still, their absence was the source of considerable soul searching and hand wringing on the bleachers website, www.section39.com. One old-timer worried that the vast popularity of the team had destroyed the spirit of the Creatures. Sheriff Tom Brown, a well-respected and particularly insightful Creature, foresaw some problems but rejected any quick-drawn conclusions.

"Today was an afternoon game, pretty much, and a lot of the regular brood was busy working or observing the Good Friday portion of Easter weekend," Brown decided. "It may not be the wild and raucous 1990s, but it is by no means the mausoleum you speak of. A lot of the tickets that used to be scarfed up by boisterous regulars are now going to Yankees front-runnin' fans, A-Rod groupies, and people who see the Yankees as an 'in thing.' Hell, even Jeter called the Yankees the 'trendy thing nowadays' and how people simply want to be seen at the Yankees game. Once we got A-Rod, I realized that tickets would be harder to score on a here-and-there basis and that the seats would be filled by first-timers, never-wases, and never-will-agains."

But the main news of the day was Torre's new contract. Torre sounded enthralled. He'd been worried that George Steinbrenner had no use for him anymore, but then there was a détente during spring training, and now Torre was feeling loved again. It was also good news for Torre's wife, Ali, a delightful woman who had now resigned herself to the fact that her husband was wedded first, and foremost, to baseball. The wives, husbands, boyfriends, and girl-friends of the Bleacher Creatures could have told Ali, from the start, there was no point in fighting such an addiction.

APRIL 23, 2004				R	H	E
	123	456	789	R	H	E
RED SOX	010	501	310	11	12	0
YANKEES	000	000	200	2	7	1

RIVALRIES AND REVELRIES

The nemesis of all Bleacher Creatures, New York undercover police officer Tom, was on the prowl again. Tom hated all Yankees fans and detested everything they symbolized. He'd grown up a Mets fan in the Bronx with a chip on his shoulder the size of his ample shaved head. These outsiders would come into his neighborhood, into his home borough, and pretend that the Yankees were somehow a part of their upbringing. They didn't really like the Yankees, Tom always figured. They only liked the championship banners. He relished his role as super villain.

"I hate the Creatures and their big mouths," Tom said. "None of them is from New York."

He loved writing up the Creatures for public drinking, for underage drinking, or for any drinking. He'd nailed them with citations during the 2003 playoffs and hunted them down after he'd chased and cuffed the kids selling knockoff Yankees souvenirs. He always made a point of complimenting the behavior of Red Sox fans. Another patrolman, Urciouli, was the same way. And on this Friday afternoon before the big Red Sox game, Urciouli was standing guard outside a parking deck, directing Boston fans to the best spaces, while Tom was enthusiastically performing his undercover work. Tom had donned a Mets jersey as his evildoer costume, the perfect bait to catch a Creature. Wearing a Mets jersey around the Bronx bleachers was like waving a red cape in front of an inebriated bull.

"Mets suck! Mets suck!" the Creatures screamed in Tom's direction, taking the bait when they spotted the jersey.

The Creatures were having another peaceful pregame barbecue, gulping some beers at a secret location announced only on their website. They were drinking from cups, so the alcohol wouldn't be obvious. Unfortunately, the cups were labeled "Bud

Tone Capone's priceless heirloom, the Babe Ruth statue, made it to the barbecue but not to the game for fear that it would be taken away by security and never returned. (Larry Palumbo/Coyote Magic Photography)

Sheriff Tom gives his signature look from the Yankee Stadium bleachers. (Larry Palumbo/Coyote Magic Photography)

Lite." Tom spun in their direction. There was a noticeable groan from the bleacherites, when he was recognized.

"Mets suck, huh?" Tom said. "Let's see some IDs."

While Tom took bureaucratic inventory, he harangued the Creatures about their rooting history, his favorite pet peeve.

"How many of you are from the city?" Tom demanded.

Steve Krauss, a.k.a. G.B. Steve, raised his hand.

"Staten Island," Steve said.

"That's not the city," the undercover cop growled. "You guys aren't real fans. How many of you can name the starting lineup of the 1990 Yankees, when they weren't worth a damn?"

A few Creatures began to recite that lineup, but Tom was in no mood to listen. He would let them off easy this time, just a few verbal warnings. He'd go after them harder late in the season, after tempers had simmered a bit. Tom departed, and the festivities began again. Nobody was happy with the way the season was going. The Yankees had lost three of four at Fenway. Several of the Creatures were on hand to watch those games, after taking the four-hour drive north. A couple of them had been tossed out of the park, in frustration.

"You don't win with All-Star teams," Bald Vinny said.

When the Yankees captured those four championships in five years, they'd done it with a balanced lineup of near stars and role players, with defense and patient hitting. They didn't have an A-Rod then, or a Giambi. They didn't need one, because the pitching and the chemistry were so fine-tuned.

Several charter members from Section 39 arrived as the barbecue hit mid-stride. Tone Capone came and brought with him a two-foot-high statue of Babe Ruth that once belonged to his great-great grandfather. Capone wanted to bring the statue into the stadium but feared that security guards would confiscate the precious knickknack. Ever since 9/11, it was impossible to carry anything into the bleachers, even such a harmless object. For all anybody knew, the Babe could be packed with plastic explosives. Stuff like this had to be checked at the local bowling alley, across the street from the stadium.

Sheriff Tom Brown (a Creature and self-appointed officer of the law, never to be confused with undercover cop Tom) was the next arrival. Sheriff Tom was perhaps the most beloved of all the Creatures. His many escapades were legend. His tongue was so sharp he often appeared as a guest on local radio talk shows. His girth had dramatically increased over the seasons. Sheriff Tom owned an insatiable thirst for both life and beer, not necessarily in that order. He'd settled down a bit, got married, and had a baby girl, Emma. He was a proud father now, bragging about how Emma was the most agile child at the playground. But the naughty Creature was still there, and so were the old tales. Tom was thrown out of Fenway once without ever entering the place, as he walked through the turnstiles. He was drunk, again, at the time.

"You can't throw me out, I'm Sheriff Tom," Brown told a police officer.

"Sheriff Tom, I'm Officer Pat, good to meet you," the policeman said. "But you can't come in."

Another time, Sheriff Tom had gone to an afternoon Yankees game with a friend and then headed out to dine at Little Italy that evening. But both men fell asleep on the subway and woke up at the last stop on the line, Coney Island. They still had time to get back for dinner at Little Italy, so they re-boarded the subway in the other direction. But they fell asleep again, only to awaken back at the Yankee Stadium station, 161st Street, four hours after they began their journey. When intoxicated, which was quite often in the old days, Sheriff Tom had been known to deputize many women in the bleachers, for purposes unknown.

A lot of the communal feelings in the bleachers started with Sheriff Tom and extended toward everyone in the group. Bald Vinny's grandmother had died of cancer this week, and a bouquet of flowers was delivered to him, courtesy of the Creatures. And when Donald Simpson showed up for the barbecue, it was a reminder of just how deep those loyalties ran.

O f all the Creatures, Simpson may have had the most compelling urban tale of all. He was a phoenix, arisen from the ashes of 9/11. On that fateful Tuesday in 2001, Simpson, a lifelong Yankees fan from Harlem and a core Creature, made his way to what would become a sadly ironic safety session at his workplace with Verizon on the 12th floor of 2 World Trade Center. Donald, Big D, was a line installer for the telephone company. The meeting was called for 8 a.m. Donald, employed in special services, got out of the session and the building about 8:30 a.m. and was beeped by his dispatch department. He fortunately chose to walk across the street before responding, because he didn't want to use a non-union phone that was closer. Suddenly, debris was falling from Tower 1. He tried to call his coworkers and warn some of them on higher floors to get out, but couldn't get to a phone. And then, another plane came from behind, from the west, to hit Tower 2.

"All of a sudden, boom, there was a bright light that threw everybody down," Donald said. "Everything went white. People were running up my back. I thought it was the end."

He was heading up Liberty Street toward Broadway when the first plane hit. He was walking back to the stricken building with a coworker when the second plane slammed into the other tower, propelling Donald into the air.

"Suddenly, I'm on the ground, on top of this lady," Donald said. "Somebody is yelling, 'Run, they're shooting into the building.'"

After the attack in true Bleacher Creature fashion, Donald stumbled toward the South Street Seaport to Jeremy's Ale House, a favorite old hangout, where beer was reasonably priced and women's lingerie hung from the ceiling like erotic spider webs. He hooked up with some friends, drank away his shock and sorrow. He drank some more with a fellow Creature on the West Side. By the time he showed up at a hospital, Donald was told to go home and get sober. That indiscretion nearly cost him any recompense for his back injuries, because the September 11 Victim Compensation Fund would have a rule that medical problems from 9/11 needed to be documented within 72 hours.

Before they had received information about their comrades, the Creatures were worried about Donald and others who worked in the area. An acrimonious band of irascible fans somehow cobbled together a communications support network to monitor and help each other during the worst of times.

"Between our message board and instant messages, we listed the missing and one by one got word that people were safe," said Bald Vinny, who saw the second plane hit while he was commuting on a No. 7 train from Queens. "It's amazing that a group like ours, with all the fighting and cliques we have, that we all came together in time of need."

Makeshift headquarters were established at Paul Kaplan's apartment and inside Jeremy's Ale House. With cell phones, e-mail, and solid detective work, the Creatures worked through the next 24 hours until virtually every one of their own had been contacted.

"One by one, all the names of the Bleacher Creatures came into question," Jessica Herold said. "Mr. Mango was off from work. Steve Krauss normally takes the Staten Island Ferry to work, which would have put him in danger, but he slept at Brian's the night before. We stayed in contact with Bald Vinny and Uptown Mike through IM [instant messaging]. Tone Capone, Grover, Walkman, MSB, and Kwik were reached by phone. No one heard from Anthony Baloo. I lit a candle and said a prayer for my friends. Finally, Baloo checked in early in the evening."

Still, there were a few Creatures missing in action. Sheriff Tom was supposed to be at work inside the World Trade Center, along with another fan, Diggity Dan. Donald had lost coworkers in the tragedy. He felt the need to return to Ground Zero. Finally, word came that Diggity Dan and Tom had been a little late for work, no surprise there, and that their tardiness might have saved their lives. Sheriff Tom Brown, the same man famous for inflicting severe emotional wounds on opposing right fielders with his merciless taunts, was spotted handing out water to victims in the streets around the World Trade Center. Even to Mets fans. Instead of checking into a hospital again, Donald and his brother, Danny, worked alongside rescue teams the whole next week. Donald received a pendant from Red Cross workers for helping so tirelessly at the site. It wasn't until afterward that Donald realized he was severely traumatized and significantly injured.

The baseball games were postponed for a few days, which was fine by everybody. Donald was clearly aching, physically and psychologically.

"I love the Yankees, and I'll take some relief being around friends," Donald said then. "But during the World Series, it's packed, the whole world is watching, you don't know for sure anymore. And you know how we complained all the time about being searched and patted down going into the bleachers? Do we still complain?"

Those who knew Donald Simpson before 9/11, and then afterward, could tell the difference immediately. He was obviously confused and hurting. He soon lost his job, his bearings.

"I had a thousand calls from the Creatures, saying, 'At least come to the games so we can see you're okay,'" Donald said.

He started going again, back up to about 60 games a year. The Yankees were a salve for his wounds. He underwent psychiatric counseling, was prescribed pain pills, and was found eligible for workers compensation as a 9/11 victim. He discovered Trial Lawyers Care, which began a long successful legal process.

Almost exactly two years after the nation's great disaster, on September 10, 2003, at the age of 43, Donald became a millionaire. A letter arrived from Kenneth Feinberg, representing the September 11th Victim Compensation Fund and U.S. Department of Justice. Because of the injuries he'd suffered two years earlier on 9/11, Donald was awarded $1.292 million—thanks, in large part, to the free legal work by attorneys David Kownacki and Brad Roskin with Trial Lawyers Care.

"We were concerned that he might not be eligible to be compensated," Kownacki said. "But we presented to the fund that he had two herniated discs, post-traumatic stress, and minor injuries—and they accepted it."

In addition to the award, the special master estimated that Donald would probably be able to collect more than $500,000 from Social Security disability awards and workers compensation. He would surely use some of that for medical expenses. Donald's doctors wanted to shave and fuse the vertebrae in his neck region, a procedure he was reluctant to undergo. He preferred simpler, temporary solutions, like buying himself a portable chair with a back for support, to slip atop the plastic bench in Section 39.

Donald accepted his $1.292 million payment in a lump sum and handed it to his father and former union leader, Donald Sr., to manage. He bought a house in upstate New York, purchased some gifts for friends, and renewed his season tickets in the bleachers. He never considered getting box seats. Money never had anything to do with the company he kept.

"That was always the one thing keeping me breathing," Donald said. "My second family in the bleachers."

Donald, a tall, good-looking African American, was still looking for romance. He wanted to start a family. He hoped to find a woman who would want him for his character, not for his bank account. Maybe there were other millionaires lurking in the bleachers, but nobody knew of them. The rich guys usually sat on the other side of the concrete gap that separated the box seats from the proud rabble in the $8 and $10 seats.

"The money is great, but I want the people back, the buildings back, my great job back," Simpson said. "I feel sometimes like I'm getting the money off the blood of other people."

When the barbecue was done, Donald and the Creatures worked their way into Section 39 for another game, for what they hoped would be some quick revenge for three losses at Fenway in a four-game series that finished badly just four days earlier. It wouldn't be so easy, though. The Yankees' All-Star lineup was still nervous, still behaving badly. Gary Sheffield and Alex Rodriguez were pressing too hard, trying to make an impression with their new team. They were veterans, but nobody was immune to pinstriped jitters. The team wasn't jelling yet, and it was unfortunate that so many games against the Red Sox were jammed into the early season like this.

Then there was the matter of the day's starter, Jose Contreras, the depressed and depressing right-hander. Contreras was moping about the clubhouse, homesick for the family he left behind in Cuba, and he was not living up to his clippings or his contract on the mound. No matter how much Yankees officials willed otherwise, Contreras didn't seem to have the stomach for the tight situation. He had plenty of stuff on his pitches, more than enough kick. He was just too fine or too frightened. Although his history against the Red Sox was brief, it was not good. This game would be no exception. Contreras was tagged for five runs in three and a third innings, and Boston went on to slam four homers in the rout. The Yankees offense never solved Derek Lowe's sinkerball, as the top four hitters in the lineup went two for 15. It was not a pleasant evening for most of the 55,001 spectators, except for the invading Red Sox fans who reveled in the one-sided game.

Whenever and wherever these two teams met, the claustrophobic geography of their rivalry meant that fans from both sides would breach enemy lines and set up camp in small color clusters of blue or red—quite often in the bleachers. The Creatures would take trips up to Fenway Park, some of them legendary. In the Bronx, the Yankee Stadium regulars would never admit to welcoming a stream of Red Sox fans into the right-field stands. But the fact remained that such an invasion inspired some of the edgiest and most passionate rooting, by both sides.

The Creatures were ready for this game, even if the Yankees weren't. At the close of the regular roll call, they chanted, "Aaron Boone," to remind the Boston fans of how the 2003 season had ended miserably for them. Then Milton unwrapped his brand new cowbell, which he'd bought for $53 and had been touting for nearly a week. Cowbells like this one, with their strong middle overtones, had gone from rural dairy farms to the city's Latin nightclubs to America's ballparks. And now a new one was in the proud hands of Milton, who didn't like to change cowbells very often. His old one was badly bashed and had run out of luck. This one wasn't doing much good, either, when he started banging out the traditional rhythms in the third inning.

The Red Sox just kept smacking homers, circling the bases. The Yankees heaped on a series of bad fielding plays. Bubba Crosby, the kid starting in center, stumbled around and allowed a fly ball to bounce in, next to him. A-Rod couldn't hit again and got booed. Derek Jeter, mired in the worst slump of his career, was jeered in the Bronx for one of the first times in his career.

"Even when they boo you, they want to cheer you," Derek would say, graciously, after the game.

Most of the Creatures went out of their way to chant his name, supportively, every time at bat. Jeter was in a terrible rut, but he wasn't the only problem. The starting rotation was struggling mightily. The Yankees were hitting just over .210 as a team, worst in the American League. As the game spiraled out of control, as it started to rain during the late innings, most of the Yankees fans in the box and reserve seats left the stadium. There were only the Creatures and the Red Sox fans left.

	1	2	3	4	5	6	7	8	9	R	H	E
A'S	2	0	0	0	0	1	1	1	0	5	10	0
YANKEES	1	0	1	0	1	3	0	1	X	7	10	0

PULLING FOR JETER

It's no picnic in the bleachers, even during the best of weather. The experience requires a firm back, a strong will, and sharp elbows. Fans sit pressed together on flat plastic benches, without clear demarcation, and they stand at a moment's notice to obstruct the view of people behind them, who stand in turn to block the people behind them, etc. There is no roof to deflect the rain, the wind, the wilting midsummer sun. This is not the best place to watch a game, if the idea is to sit in comfort and to savor every pitch. What is heaven for some is purgatory for others.

In the not-so-old days, back in 1996, Section 39 was sparsely populated on most nights. A Creature could spread out a bit, pass around some snacks, drink beer, and relax. But now, more than 2.9 million tickets were sold to the 81 home games at Yankee Stadium, even before the season started. Another million fans were still making similar plans for 2004, opening their wallets at the box office or ordering tickets over the Internet. Too many of those spectators were headed to the right-field stands. As Section 39 gained in notoriety, the area was becoming a mosh pit. Bleachers fans came to sit in Section 39, even if their tickets said Section 41 or 43. As a result, the plastic benches were overrun by both interlopers and by old favorites. On a stretch of bench where two people were supposed to sit, there were often three or four. On top of this claustrophobic crowd, a gaggle of police and security guards roamed the region. Vendors wriggled their way through. And when things got wild, which was most of the time, the squeeze was on and bodies banged together. If it wasn't Paul Kaplan rolling from row to row during the seventh inning—a painful ritual Kaplan abandoned when he lost considerable weight and body padding—it could just be Bald Vinny leading the roll call or Milton getting people riled up with the cowbell.

So it required considerable vigor and good health to be part of this ragged fun, and Tina Lewis said she still wasn't ready. On the phone, she predicted she would be out there in a few days for her season debut and that her doctor would give her clearance by then. Tina was plotting her return to her throne, to Section 39, Row A, Seat 29. She said a change of hairstyle was in the offing.

Meanwhile, she was pulling for Derek Jeter. Jeter was mired in an amazing slump by now, a zero for 32 streak that was the worst by a Yankee since 1977. In the clubhouse before the game, Jeter was getting dressed while Luis was running around doing favors for A-Rod. It appeared that Luis's new laundry responsibilities did not necessarily provide him immunity from gofer duties. Luis was too efficient, too cordial, and too bilingual for his own good. Jeter was always nice to him. Derek could be slick and guarded with reporters, but he was as even-tempered as they got. The Yankees shortstop was smiling and joking around, despite the slump. He was hoping to find some kind of regimen that would break his run of miserable luck.

It was 3:45 p.m. when Jeter walked to his locker and called Ruben Sierra "a canary," employing an odd Spanish accent. Sierra demanded to know why Jeter called him that, and Jeter went to great jovial lengths to explain the origin of the nickname.

"Start hitting the ball," Sierra said, walking away.

It was hard to tell whether he was joking. Hopefully, he was.

At 4:02 p.m., Jeter headed through a tunnel from the clubhouse to the field, past a General Douglas MacArthur quote posted at the orders of George Steinbrenner, for extra batting practice. Four coaches, including Don Mattingly, and teammates were watching. Jeter mostly hit to the opposite field, lining four balls over the wall in right, where the Creatures would start arriving in about 90 minutes. The swing looked marvelous, like it belonged to a lifetime .315 hitter with more postseason hits than anybody in history. It did.

At 4:15 p.m., Jeter walked back to his locker to face the press for a pregame debriefing. He answered questions until there were no more questions. He laughed about having passed Willie

Randolph, at zero for 30, about being tied with Yogi Berra, at zero for 32. He said he was swinging the bat well, that he was doing nothing differently. He appreciated the sympathy from fans, and all the tips in his mailbag. But...

"You start changing things, you go crazy," he said.

While Jeter talked, and as Luis scooted past on yet another errand, there were two black autographed bats standing upright behind Jeter, crossed at the handles.

While Jeter did calisthenics, Joe Torre sat in the dugout and said he would never sit his shortstop down for a game, "because I don't think he'd be fun to be around."

Torre said Jeter had to keep his front shoulder from flying open. He had to try to go the other way. It's nothing more complicated than that, the manager said.

"Just one of those ugly streaks," Torre said. "If there's anybody I would pick who could handle it emotionally, it would be Derek."

At 4:55 p.m., Jeter stepped to the plate for more batting practice. He was pulling the ball and was less impressive this time. When he was done, at 5:02 p.m., Reggie Jackson had his minute with Jeter and offered a few more tips. Jackson would tell reporters later the key to breaking a slump like this was proper off-field love-making. No wonder Reggie was always a favorite with the Bleacher Creatures. It was 5:10 p.m. when Jeter walked back into the clubhouse to prepare for the game. He ducked briefly into the trainer's room. Were his fingers aching? He wouldn't tell anybody.

"I'm fine," he said over and over.

It was 7:01 p.m. when Jeter took his shortstop position and stood for the national anthem. He tipped his glove to the Creatures when they chanted his name during the roll call. It was 7:15 p.m., and the Yankees already were down two runs when he threw out Jermaine Dye on a grounder to short. It was 7:16 p.m. when he snagged a liner by Scott Hatteberg to end the first inning. It was a perfect fielding play, but nobody came for the fielding. It was 7:19 p.m. when Jeter stepped into the batter's box to a standing ovation from the bleachers and from everywhere else in the old park. The whole place was chanting his name.

Jeter smacked the first pitch, a fat fastball from Barry Zito, over the left-center wall into Monument Park for a homer. Jeter smiled and waved.

"A streak like that you wouldn't wish on anyone," he said later.

The Yanks went on to win and, in the bleachers, there was a prescient belief that the worst was over for everyone, including Jeter.

The Creatures had an odd relationship with the Yankees shortstop. They understood his importance to the team and his history of success and seemed to rally around Jeter at times like these. But Jeter was not quite Bernie Williams to them. There were nights when the Creatures would actually chant, "No-mar's better," comparing Jeter unkindly to the Red Sox shortstop. Jeter didn't patrol the outfield near the bleachers, the way Bernie did, and he seemed a bit more aloof in general. There was that other thing, too: Jeter was a bit too good looking. Few of the fans in Section 39 wore Jeter's No. 2 jersey because of that factor. Milton Ousland was the exception.

"I have no shame in wearing a Jeter shirt," Milton said. "Girls are supposed to wear it. Guys don't want to be chanting Jeter's name. I know. I take a lot of grief. I've argued about it a thousand times. But there's something about him. It's not about the stats. He brings such confidence, an aura. He's the straw that stirs the drink, like Reggie was."

Milton was always sure that Jeter would snap out of his slump and that he just needed to become accustomed to the presence of Rodriguez. The home run on this night made Milton surer.

```
MAY 16, 2004                                    (22-15)

                  123  456  789      R  H  E
MARINERS          000  000  010      1  9  0
YANKEES           001  100  00X      2  5  0
```

THE
QUEEN
RETURNS

Two hours before game time Tina arrived at the No. 4 train station ready for her first game of the season. She looked great. Even at 42, Tina seemed unchanging and ageless. She said doctors had pronounced her cancer-free. She'd had a makeover and not just from the radiation treatments. Her friend and fellow Creature, Evelyn, had cut and styled her hair back in Jersey, ribboned in some highlights among the tight red curls. She wore festive Yankees-blue toenail polish.

In 2003 doctors had found two cancerous tumors on the top of her head in May, which had been causing her headaches. She underwent surgery in June and then received 27 radiation treatments during the season to eradicate all the bad cells. Doctors told her she would have been a goner if she'd waited 30 more days to be examined. Tina missed about 25 Yankees games because of the medical appointments, and that was torture of a different sort. During her lowest moments, Tina started wondering who should inherit her prestigious Row A seat on the aisle, Ali's seat, if she didn't make it. She confided at the time that it should be Mike Donahue, a particularly irrepressible Creature, but Tina didn't want to make her choice public for fear of the controversy. Such a decision was bound to create even more political in-fighting among the Creatures, already well known for their intramural spats and rigid pecking order. Newcomers had to pay their dues and would always be identified by the year in which they first showed up in the bleachers. They were '98ers, or '99ers. And they were forever held in lower regard, even disdain, from those with greater seniority. But now it wasn't an issue. She was back.

"I'm strong," Tina said. "Not on my deathbed."

She had some personal problems, though, enough to super-sede her cancer worries and to erode her stomach lining. Tina's nomadic existence had caught up with her. She was too distracted to do the one thing she loved most, which was hanging outside the press entrance in the late afternoons, waiting for the players to walk past and sign autographs. This was the one place where the Creatures interacted directly with the athletes, where the fans learned a bit more about the personalities of the stars they adored. There weren't many such opportunities on the field, except for brief gestures of appreciation or hostility (a Detroit pitcher once wrote, "Bleachers suck," on a baseball and threw it at the Creatures). And there weren't many chances in real life, either, except for a few serendipitous moments—like the time when several bleachers fans were riding back on the No. 7 subway from a depressing Yankees loss to the Mets at Shea, complaining about the play of Nick Johnson, only to discover that Johnson was sitting in the same train car. Apologies were accepted, and many photos were taken.

Bernie Williams was always Tina's favorite. Bernie was an incredibly engaging and considerate guy, a baseball player with a musician's soul. He would often acknowledge the fans at the press gate, occasionally stopping to chat. Two years earlier, he bothered to ask Tina why the Creatures had temporarily suspended their first-inning roll call. Tina explained to Williams that it was a protest against the get-tough policy by Yankees officials who had cracked down on profane chants and minor infractions in the bleachers. Tina didn't support the roll-call suspension. She thought the new rules were reasonable. Bernie listened to her patiently. Another time, he went down to the clubhouse and had one of the attendants bring Tina his jazz-guitar CD. The album was autographed.

It went this way for years, these delightful experiences, and then her illness and her complicated life had sabotaged everything. Clearly, Tina needed some bleachers time to clear her head. She had been away from the place for far too long. Just being near the River Avenue entrance brought back wonderful memories for her, and she soon began to calm down, to enjoy the perfect day, and to remember how she first arrived at the bleachers.

Tina Lewis is the self-proclaimed "queen of the bleachers." She loves the Yankees and finds herself most at home in her seat in Section 39. (Larry Palumbo/Coyote Magic Photography)

Tina saw her first baseball game at age three, when her brother took her to Tiger Stadium in Detroit, where she grew up. The Tigers were playing the Yankees, and for some reason Tina immediately loved the team wearing the gray road uniforms. She started going to the bleachers, sitting on the third-base line at Yankee Stadium in 1977, after it was renovated for the last time. She kept hearing the powerful siren call of Ali Ramirez's cowbell and wondered what it must be like in the right-field bleachers.

Then on July 4, 1983, she went there and found out. Dave Righetti pitched a no-hitter on that holiday, and Tina never strayed too far from Section 39 again—except for the very occasional road trip. She had a temper. Tina considered herself a volatile Albanian American. Her maiden name before 11 years of marriage was Lulgjuraj. It wasn't always wise for her to travel behind enemy lines. She proudly recounted that game at Shea Stadium in 1999, when the Yankees were playing her most hated team, the Mets. She got in a nasty argument with a Mets fan. He called her a name.

"I slapped him," Tina said. "And then I slapped him again when the policeman came."

She was thrown out of Shea, a badge of honor in her book. Tina often talked about fumigating the bleachers whenever a Mets fan visited, uninvited. That was her favorite line.

Her ongoing feud with Mets continued outside of the bleachers as well. In the real world, she had been employed, on and off, as a counter server at several delis and diners. When she worked at Champs, in the financial district of New York, her boss Vinny (not to be confused for bleachers mainstay, Bald Vinny) had fired her more times than George Steinbrenner fired Billy Martin. She had an eternal battle with Mets fans there, particularly one customer named Neil who loved to get her goat as he walked past the sandwich section. Neil wore his Mets cap in line and mumbled bad things about the Yankees, knowing full well that Tina would not be able to keep hold of her emotions. So there were occasional problems.

But Vinny liked Tina and helped her out whenever he could. That included finding for her the perfect viewing window, above the restaurant, where Tina and her friends could watch the passing Yankees championship parades nearly every October during the late 1990s.

Tina may have been down on her luck, but she had her dignity.

"Because of the way I look, tough, sometimes people in Yankee Stadium will look at me and say, 'Go drink another beer, you wino,'" Tina said. "But I don't drink and I tell them to respect me. I'm just as good as you. Respect me as a fan. I can help you."

By October 2003, Tina's cancer was in remission and the Yanks made her very happy with a seventh-game victory over the Red Sox in the American League Championship Series. She couldn't come to many postseason games, though. The October nights were too long, too cold, and too wearing.

"You know something's got to be really wrong with me for me not to be going," Tina said then. "I'm not 100 percent. My white cells are going every way, except the way they're supposed to. I'm all right; don't worry. But this is just too much pressure for me to go through, yet."

Tina didn't watch Game 7 against the Red Sox, not even on television. She really couldn't enjoy Aaron Boone's homer, because she had been in the hospital earlier that day for tests and treatment. She went to her friend Evelyn's house, and Evelyn came in where Tina was resting to tell her that the Yankees had come all the way back to win Game 7 in extra innings. Tina had already suspected as much, because she could hear the horns honking outside, a wall of happy street noise. She and Evelyn hailed a cab, and they rode around the city waving a Yankees banner.

"I'm just glad we got rid of those idiots from Boston," Tina said. "I couldn't take the idea of them celebrating in our home."

That was the way Tina left the 2003 season, an unfinished symphony of car horns.

Ali's seat. This plaque is dedicated to the original cowbell man, who died May 8, 1996. (Larry Palumbo/Coyote Magic Photography)

On this May afternoon, Tina bumped into a lot of friends on a walk along River Avenue. There was one of the twins—she couldn't figure out which one—who ran a sandwich shop called, aptly enough, Twins. The shop was stuck in a little alley, dwarfed by Stan's giant emporium. Twins appeared to be an unofficial snack bar and souvenir stand. It occasionally was closed down over one zoning ordinance or another. Later in the year, it would be shut down for good. The twins, John and Joe, would then operate a 24-hour diner in New Jersey, the Yellow Rose in Keyport, each one working 12-hour shifts, so that the general public believed there was just one owner who never took a minute's break.

Stan's remained an intimidating empire on River Avenue, stretched out for nearly an entire city block. Stan's two kids were now running the operation. One ruled the tavern; the other supervised the clothes outlets. Bald Vinny set up shop every night in front of the tavern, with his improvised T-shirt stand. He was renting space from Stan's on the sidewalk, and he would stash his inventory in the bar minutes before game time so that he could run into the bleachers to start the first-inning roll call. Vinny, always the entrepreneur, had a couple new models. He had shirts

Statman shows off his work and does what he does best. He is the official score-keeper of the bleachers. (Larry Palumbo/Coyote Magic Photography)

that said, "Section 37," to go along with the ones that read, "Section 39." He was debating whether to start producing shirts for Section 41, Section 43, ad infinitum.

Tina was anxious to get to her seat in the bleachers.

"It's been too long," she said.

When she reached her bench, she checked the bronze memorial plaque on her seat, the one for Ali. She wiped it with a towel, reverentially. After a while, some of the Creatures filed in for the game, and Tina quickly forgot all that ailed her. Monica hugged Tina. Norma hugged her, before Norma screamed at her Section 37 nemesis, Iris, not to start anything.

"I'm already the old Tina," Tina announced.

Terence Williams, the amiable security guard, smiled and chatted with her. Terence was the only Mets fan that Tina would abide. He tried to keep his rooting interest secret, but it didn't matter really. He was too nice a guy for any of the Creatures to hold against him that peculiar personality flaw.

Not long ago, before the arrival of season tickets and numbered benches, these bleacher seats were supposed to go to fans on a first-come, first-serve basis. That wasn't satisfactory to the regulars, who needed to reserve about 40 seats for themselves. So it became the job of rookie Creatures, like Walkman John, to get to the park early and shoo away unwanted interlopers from the area. Now, the Yankees sold these bleachers seats in a variety of ticket packages. There was the 46-game package, which included almost no weekend games but guaranteed access to playoff tickets. There was the 61-game package, which threw in a few more showcase games. There was the full-blown 81-game package. Most of the core Creatures went for the 46-game deal, for obvious financial reasons. That meant that on a gorgeous Sunday afternoon like this one, there were only a few of the old regulars on hand. Walkman John was one of them. He had a job now with the Elias Sports Bureau, compiling statistics. This was the perfect deal for him. John had been compulsive about his scorekeeping, nearly as committed as the bleachers' official scorer, Statman. Since Walkman John got his job, he attended fewer Yankees games and worried less about a complete 81-game scorecard collection. But on this day, Walkman John was off work, and he was ready to go.

"I have to say, this is a lot healthier for me, to have other things in my life," Walkman John said.

Statman was still going strong, though, undeterred by any of life's distractions. Normally, he sat in Section 37, but for now he was seated in front of Tina, radio earphones already in place, his thick glasses glued to today's virgin score card. It spread out before him, tantalizing in all its empty, symmetrical squares, full of potential plot twists. Nobody kept score as neatly and meticulously as Statman. He was a groundskeeper at an apartment project in Queens, and he treated his piece of paper like one of his manicured lawns. Nobody ever bothered to call him by his real name, Steve Tipa. Statman was able to recite any statistic and to recall any game situation from any era upon demand. Or, at times, without demand.

"We were beaten by a Putz yesterday," he suddenly declared.

Statman could not get over the notion that reliever J.J. Putz of Seattle had shut down the Yankees during a 13-7 Mariners victory in extra innings.

The Yanks had fared much better of late, despite that one loss to Seattle. With a victory today, they would win their sixth straight series. The humiliation of those Boston losses back in April had quickly melted away, along with a four-and-a-half-game deficit in the standings. The Red Sox were losing more than their share of games. The Yanks were leapfrogging back and forth with Boston for the lead in the AL East. The way it looked now, this jockeying would continue right through September.

The Yanks, at least most of them, had started to hit. A-Rod broke out, already up to .290, and there were a couple of big comeback games recently in which the Yanks wiped out six-run deficits. The middle relief, a disaster in 2003, had kept opponents from scoring those nail-in-the-coffin runs that put games away. That was the good news.

But Derek Jeter was still hitting .195 and Bernie Williams was at .228. Jorge Posada's nose was broken, after a relay throw from second caught him in the face while he was sliding into the bag trying to break up a double play. Then there was the high-priced starting rotation, which was one of the worst in the league, at least statistically. Kevin Brown was fine. Javier Vazquez and Mike Mussina had been inconsistent. After that, everyone was consistently lousy. Jose Contreras would be sent down to Tampa for some more minor-league tuning.

The Creatures, spoiled rotten by George Steinbrenner, were unconcerned. They continued to believe the Yanks would win a Randy Johnson bidding war and add him by midseason. The Diamondbacks had started off terribly, and a fire sale seemed inevitable. Bald Vinny thought aloud how great it would be if Johnson ended up pitching against Curt Schilling in Game 7 of another playoff series against the Red Sox at the stadium. That was a long way off though. The Yanks would need to win the division first to gain homefield advantage.

The game started. Tina settled into her seat and immediately booed Kenny Lofton. Lofton was playing center today instead of Williams, who was resting.

"Where's Bernie?" Tina yelled. "I don't like Lofton."

Tina didn't like Lofton because he was a part-time replacement for Williams, and she didn't like Jason Giambi because he had arrived two years earlier at first base to replace another of her favorites, Tino Martinez. The other Yankees were all in her favor at the moment.

The Mariners were in town, which meant Ichiro Suzuki would be in right field for Seattle, and that he would be playing against the other Japanese legend, Hideki Matsui. Each time this happened, it was quite the occasion back in Japan, where these two teams were very popular and where their games were often broadcast at all hours of the early morning. Japan's ambassador to the United States was a guest today, walking to the mound for the ceremonial first pitch. He staged an exaggerated windup and then delivered a near strike. There was more than the usual number of Japanese-American fans in attendance, too. In the bleachers, one of them started a chant for "Mat-sy" when Matsui came to the plate. The Creatures chanted, "Home run, Matsui!" a funny, Japanese-American sounding hybrid of a cheer. Many of the Creatures had memorized some nasty Japanese phrases, which they sent in Ichiro's direction now and then. Even Tina remembered a couple, and she was no language scholar.

MAY 29

DONALD'S NEW HOME

The Yankees were finishing up their longest road trip of the season—a successful 12-game swing that zigzagged west, then east, and then south—when the invitation came by e-mail: Donald Simpson was holding an open house for all Creatures and family at his new home in Brewster, New York. The party would be staged on a glorious Saturday afternoon at the start of the Memorial Day weekend to mark Donald's rite of passage into home ownership. There was free food and drink at a nearby clubhouse, which made the hour-plus drive north from the city far more tempting. Steve Krauss, a.k.a. G.B. Steve, ventured all the way from Staten Island, nearly two hours, bringing Midget Mike along. The place was so idyllic, not even Midget Mike could find a reason to complain as he pointed out a turtle in a pond.

"There it is, see it?" Midget Mike said, sounding about eight years old.

It was odd seeing the bleachers denizens in such a bucolic setting, ogling turtles, far from River Avenue and the elevated subway. But they were adaptable Creatures, if nothing else. Donald was proof of that.

There were people in the New York region who resented Donald for getting his sizable award from the 9/11 victims fund, which ended up giving more than 5,000 families nearly $7 billion. After my column about his windfall, some e-mailers complained that he shouldn't receive the money that would be better to send it to the families of firemen and policemen. He was also attacked on at least one website. But those who knew Donald personally knew better. He had suffered terribly, physically and psychologically, since the World Trade Center attack. A lot of the joy had gone out of the man, and he was truly disoriented for more than a year. His closest acquaintances worried for him and worked behind the scenes on his behalf.

On most days, Donald spent a large portion of the time flat on his back or in a position to ease the back pain he was suffering since 2001. For this open house, though, he would take his role as host seriously enough to muster the energy to stay upright for nearly 12 straight hours. It wasn't easy for him. But as friends arrived at irregular intervals to his new townhouse in the isolated Fieldstone Pond development, Donald patiently and proudly offered tour after tour of his new digs. He had moved very far from his native Harlem and had done a remarkable job of filling and decorating the place with a modern touch. Here was the kitchen, with a state-of-the-art fridge. Here was the bedroom, with sleek entertainment system and imported wooden bed from Germany. Here was the basement, complete with modern foldout bar. And here, the real treasure, was the Yankees Room. The second of two bedrooms had been sacrificed for this sacred purpose and dedicated in its entirety to the Bronx Bombers. The décor and furnishings were done in Yankees blue. The plush rug, too, was Yankees blue. Photos of Creatures adorned the wall, along with signed baseballs. Donald's favorite was the one autographed by Billy Martin and Thurman Munson. There were Yankees paintings and Yankees montages and Yankees banners. And if you snapped your beer cap with Donald's bottle opener, the little tool would break into announcer John Sterling's rendition of a Yankees grand slam home run. The Creatures gaped a bit at all of this. The economic demographics of the bleachers varied to some extent, from subsistence existence to rock-solid middle class. But these furnishings were something more than that, befitting Section 39's only known millionaire.

Donald was feeling particularly happy today. There were a million reasons that had little to do with dollars. He was moving into a new phase of his life, yet he was surrounded by old friends and family. Then there were the Yanks, who were playing well on the road (they'd finish the trip 8-4) and would move back past the Red

Sox into first place by nightfall. Derek Jeter and Bernie Williams had finally broken out of their slumps. The crisis had largely past.

Regardless of the opponent, the Yanks as a whole appeared far sharper than when they were stumbling around at the start of the season, fiddling with their chemical makeup. Joe Torre, master psychologist, voiced a silo full of rationalizations as to why the team had been humbled so badly by the Red Sox back in April. He said they weren't "emotionally ready" and that A-Rod, Gary Sheffield, and Javier Vazquez were trying to prove too much to the world. Sheffield was just getting used to American League pitching, Torre hypothesized, and Jeter was "squeezing the sawdust out of the bat," one of the manager's favorite sayings.

For whatever reasons, the Yankees were now playing much better. Even the starting rotation, bolstered by Jon Lieber's surprising run of success, was becoming reliable enough. The Yanks would return home on Tuesday, back to the Bronx, with momentum on their side. Donald was looking forward to that. Donald also had received good financial news, just the day before. He was eligible for full disability payments, and his union rep informed him the company would capitulate and forward all that was owed. His financial future was assured, even if there was chronic pain.

Donald's family trickled into his party, telling tales of Donald's conversion to Yankee-ism. Donald Sr., his father and a former union rep, was a proud and tall African American who wore a pin that said, "Dissent is patriotic." He remembered how his own father—Donald's grandfather—had brought him to Yankee Stadium as a young boy to watch a doubleheader with the Black Yankees, a Negro League team. Those were his first games, but Donald Sr. soon became a regular in the bleachers, paying 50 cents to watch the white Yankees of DiMaggio and Mantle.

"We sat almost exactly where Section 39 is today," Donald Sr. said. "When I started taking Donald, we had enough money to sit in better seats."

Growing up, Donald was spoiled rotten in the general admission seats, before rediscovering his roots in the right-field bleachers. Sometimes, he would drag his father, his brother, and his brother-in-law, Troy, to Section 39. Troy was a Mets fan and had to put up with some serious taunting from the Creatures. Donald Sr. said there was this one woman—what was her name, Donald Sr. tried to recall… Tina something?—who had threatened to punch out one of the Simpson clan right there in right field, if he didn't stop rooting for the Mets. Nobody could just stop rooting for a team, of course. Troy had grown up around Queens, poor fellow. Too close to Shea.

The party moved along. Donald, finding the energy from somewhere, introduced people and posed with his family and friends for photos. It was good to see him like this. The solitude of his new house would help him heal, but there was one worry. The long commute to Yankee Stadium might discourage his attendance at a time when Donald needed to be among friends to feel strongest.

The party wound down, and then it was time to head home and prepare for the next homestand. The Orioles, those dependable patsies, were scheduled for another round of pounding.

```
                 123  456  789     R H E
ORIOLES          500  000  000     5 9 3
YANKEES          300  012  00X     6 3 3
```

A SENSE OF
PRIDE

During the seventh-inning stretch at the stadium, the Yanks launched a lengthy, solemn patriotic ritual like clockwork. This was not to be confused with Paul Kaplan's unsanctioned roll through the aisles in the bleachers, which the then-rotund Bleacher Creature performed with great passion and reckless abandon throughout the late 1990s. There was not anything like that anymore. Ever since 9/11, the Yankees took great pains to stage demonstrations of nationalism on a grand scale. Other major league teams rolled back such displays a bit, reserving them for special occasions, for Sunday afternoons or for holidays. The Yankees continued to go full-bore ahead on all days and nights. George Steinbrenner was the world's most public patriot, and a man who would greatly like us all to forget his felony conviction for illegal contributions to Richard Nixon's campaign. So during this seventh-inning stretch, there was a moment of silence recalling all war casualties and then a sometimes lengthy rendition of "God Bless America." It was a bit over the top for many fans, but others seemed to enjoy the pomp that now preceded "Take Me Out to the Ball Game" and, more painfully, "Cotton Eyed Joe." During the playoffs, the between-innings break could extend to seven-plus minutes, causing the arms of opposing pitchers to stiffen and the teeth of opposing managers to gnash with impatience.

In Section 39, most of the fans had come to enjoy the extended ritual, adopting it as their own.

"You're talking New York, 9/11," Milton said. "There are a lot of proud people out here. You only get angry when you have a guy taking three and a half minutes to sing a one-minute song."

Whenever the Creatures went to Shea Stadium for a Yankees–Mets series, they would make a point of singing "God Bless America" during the seventh-inning stretch, at the top of

Bald Ray; Milton, the cowbell man; and Tina Lewis hold up the American flag during the rendition of "God Bless America" during the seven-inning stretch. (Larry Palumbo/Coyote Magic Photography)

their lungs, even though there was no music to accompany them. The visiting Creatures often got a standing ovation for their efforts, the only time that the Mets fans in Flushing recognized a truce between the two sides.

The man playing the roll of emcee for these proceedings was Bob Sheppard, the platinum-throated announcer. It was hard to describe the timbre of Sheppard's utterances, except to say that when you heard him announce anything—from the starting line-up to stern warnings about throwing stuff on the field—the words appeared to float down directly from God himself. Sheppard had been the public address announcer at Yankee Stadium since 1951, when this very formal man was hired very informally to work as many games as his teaching schedule would allow.

"A temporary job that has lasted a half century," Sheppard called the gig.

After all these years of covering the Yankees, I have yet to see Sheppard actually deliver his pronouncements firsthand. I only know he supposedly sits in a room where nobody is allowed to enter. But on this occasion, I somehow spotted him walking around behind the press box, heading for the bathroom, even while his words were echoing throughout the stadium about honoring those who had given their lives in wartime. Sheppard was not live! He was on tape! This was exactly the sort of disturbing revelation that a sportswriter must regularly experience in exchange for backstage access. A loss of innocence is inevitable, as every crack is exposed. We see the ugly innards of otherwise magnificent Yankee Stadium.

There is a cruel rule of thumb that seems to dictate that the closer one gets to the game of baseball, the more cynical he or she becomes, like a disinterested resident in paradise. The gloss is gone, and a negative view pervades everything once cherished and held dear as a fan. But in the case of Luis Castillo, the clubhouse attendant and former Bleacher Creature, it was both surprising and refreshing to see that he had somehow retained a bit of wonder about the game. Here was a young man who had literally seen the dirty laundry inside the clubhouse yet retained considerable wonder about the sport. Luis was happier this season than he had been in 2003. His job description was more flexible, and the players were easier on him. He had real bounce to his step again. There were red highlights in his hair. He had traveled down the previous week to Baltimore on his own, just to watch the Yankees play the Orioles. He would do this sometimes for road games, to Boston or to other commutable stadiums, even though his job required him to watch 81 games a year at Yankee Stadium. He did it because he loved baseball and because he really liked these players. Some of them, frankly, didn't even notice him. But there were others who did, who cared for the kid from the Bronx. There had been Ramiro Mendoza, the former Yankees reliever, who always had a kind word. And there was always David Cone, the best of all.

"He still calls me all the time," Luis was saying about Cone, before the game. "He's just a great guy."

The Yankees clubhouse before the game this day bustled with businesslike activity. The Yankees were hot, having gone 23-8 since that rocky start. The standings were starting to take their inevitable shape. The season was less than a third done, and already it appeared inevitable that both the Yanks and Red Sox would make the playoffs. The A's and Mariners had been disappointing in the AL West, and they were really the only threats to steal a wildcard spot in the postseason.

It was amazing, if you thought about it: There were kids graduating from high school in and around New York who would have a hard time remembering back before 1995, when the Yankees began their streak of qualifying for the playoffs every year. Some postseason activity was pretty much assumed now with the franchise, and this season was beginning to look like a more robotic excursion than usual.

There were just a few marginal questions, which included the mental health of fifth starter Jose Contreras. He was a mess, and the fans were losing patience with him. It was easy for a writer to say that Contreras deserved some compassion, but spectators paid a lot of money for their tickets and saw an underachieving pitcher who was given millions of dollars and seemed incapable of winning 10 games.

So the fans jeered Contreras again this particular evening, when he gave up five runs (only one earned) and never made it out of the first inning. The rude goodbye probably wasn't constructive, considering Contreras's fragile state of mind and the paltry help he received from teammates. His broad shoulders were sagging at the moment; his back was bowed. Sometimes his pace slowed painfully, and he appeared lost, like a small boy. He didn't need another kick in the rear. He threw 44 pitches all together and got way too cute. There were two errors, three walks, and a wild pitch. Enrique Wilson threw a potential double-play relay past Derek Jeter into left field. Joe Torre walked to the mound to reclaim the ball, as slowly as Contreras had delivered those pitches. Tanyon Sturtze came on for another of these big Yankees comebacks that had been the norm lately. They were especially the norm, out of necessity, whenever Contreras started.

"It's normal they boo me," he would say later, after the game. "I'd boo me, too."

Contreras was a soft-spoken, sad figure in the Yankees clubhouse, nothing like what the Yankees bargained for when they paid him $32 million over four years. There was no joy when he threw, no joy when he didn't. Contreras was trying to get through each start the way he was trying to get through each day, without his family back in Cuba, still a stranger in a land where they razzed you for yielding one earned run in the first inning. The Yankees kept sending the Cuban right-hander down to Florida for tuneups, then declaring him cured of all that ailed him. He pitched seven nice innings against Buffalo or Norfolk in the Triple-A, and his mechanics were supposed to be aligned, his head straightened. Joe Torre talked about his great stuff, but the stuff didn't go over the plate often enough.

"He didn't seem like he had any of his pitches working for him tonight," Jorge Posada said.

Half the world was playing amateur psychiatrist with this guy, especially in the stands. There was no doubt that he was confused, hurting. Contreras got upset at the mere mention of his wife and two daughters back in Cuba. He told writers to stay away from that topic, that their reports would only make political matters worse. He was furious at the *Daily News*, in particular, over a sympathetic interview of his wife that was set up at a hotel in Havana. Contreras didn't care about the content of the story. He just didn't want his wife speaking publicly, roiling the waters.

He was no Orlando Hernandez. "El Duque" was always able to separate the torn fabric of his personal life from the game on the field. Hernandez had a million stories of how he came to America from Cuba, leaving behind his own family. He was a hero. He was a deserter. He was a great mystery to everyone. But then he would step on the rubber, and there were no worries anymore, especially in the postseason. "El Duque" blocked it all out, became Señor Octubre. He didn't think about anything except the next breaking pitch. Contreras was more complicated, more of a mortal. You saw the pain on his face when he sat at his locker after a game like this, dressed in deceptively casual style, in yellow shirt and blue jeans. You wondered if he would come here again to America if he had the choice, even for all that money.

But the Yankees won again, despite Contreras, because they got great middle relief and had all their hitting going again. The Yanks drew more than 50,000 for a midweek game against the mediocre Orioles.

The Creatures were in midseason form. Tina had become a regular again, although she was still missing from the pregame masses lining outside the players' entrance. There wasn't much point to going there these days, anyway. The Yankees players were scooting past fans faster than ever, and the barricades were getting farther away from the entryway. The days when Tina could share a pregame discussion with Bernie Williams were probably past. Such was the price of unending success and mounting popularity. Tina was happy enough now cheering from her roost in Section 39, a long way from home plate.

A WAVE OF DISSENT

There is nothing more insulting to a true baseball fan than The Wave—that undulating, distracting, and feeble demonstration of self-importance by casual, uncommitted spectators. A dozen fans in some remote section of the stadium take great pride in starting the thing. They stand up in unison, throwing their arms up in the air, then sit again, anxiously watching until the gesture travels 360 degrees and it is their section's turn again. There is no interaction with the players in this gimmick, not at all like Section 39's roll call. There is no connection with anything that is happening on the field. Quite the contrary, The Wave practically demands that a fan ignore the ball game taking place in front of him in order to concentrate on the nonsensical pattern of standing and sitting in the stands.

The Bleacher Creatures hated The Wave for all these reasons and probably for a few more. They didn't invent the thing, for one. For another, the box seaters seemed to enjoy it, which is all you really had to know. The Creatures were standing half the time anyway, whether or not it was Section 39's turn to stand. So whenever The Wave reached the bleachers, the Creatures sat down and protested by extending their middle fingers, upright, in harmonious conjunction. The Finger was a fine tradition in its own right at Yankee Stadium, a counterattack on The Wave, deserving of national recognition. But suddenly, security forces in the bleachers had begun cracking down on the practice.

The problem was that TV cameras, servicing both the YES network and the scoreboard in center field, would pan the crowd during The Wave. And there on TV, or on the big board, would be a horrifying shot of those indignant and allegedly vulgar fingers in the bleachers. It wasn't the first time the club was embarrassed by the Creatures' spontaneous acts of rebellion. Recently, during

The Bleacher Creatures taunt The Wave with their own personalized gesture.
(Larry Palumbo/Coyote Magic Photography)

Steinbrenner's solemn seventh-inning ceremonies, yet another close-up of an American flag suddenly revealed a profane T-shirt (boasting of a sex act with somebody's mother), below the country's sacred symbol. And yes, this T-shirt inhabited the right-field bleachers.

When Yankees brass caught sight of The Finger, word was sent along to security to stop the ritual before another knuckle was raised. Three days before the Wednesday game against Colorado, during a Sunday afternoon game, officers ejected several of the non-regulars as a message to everybody else to stop the digital protest. Feathers were ruffled. Even Tina, who didn't participate in The Finger protest, was annoyed at such an unwarranted crackdown.

"We don't need this babysitting," she grumped.

She would put in a call to Sonny Hight, the vice president of administration for the Yankees. Tina considered Sonny to be something of a protector. He had intervened on behalf of the Creatures in the past, she said. It was time again. The Creatures felt their inalienable rights to freedom of speech and the consumption of alcohol had slowly eroded over the past decade, and this was just another step in the wrong direction.

As with every other ban, there would be ways around this latest regulation, once the bleacherites focused their imaginative minds on the problem. The biggest challenge of all had been the stunning alcohol ban in 2000. Back then, the Creatures arrived at their beloved bleachers to discover two new blue signs stuck to the outer wall along River Avenue. One read, "Bleachers are now alcohol free." The other, "Intoxicated fans will not be permitted into the Stadium." The first was annoying, a breach of sacred civil rights. The second was just plain ridiculous, because it wasn't going to be enforceable. Two bucks at the Associated Supermarket on 161st got you an extra-large Colt .45 before the game. Four bucks got you two. And so on, and so forth.

"The next thing, they're going to make us all wear ties, and they'll start broadcasting the games in black and white," groused Sheriff Tom Brown, blood-alcohol level unknown at the time of the ban. "I'm going to bring every four-year-old I know with an Incredible Hulk lunchbox. You can sneak a six-pack in that thing. Maybe I'll get me a hollowed-out wooden leg."

The Creatures harbored an undying belief that beer doesn't heckle people. People heckle people.

"We're baking out here in the sun, and we need that cold beer more than anybody else," Donald Simpson said.

Tina never touched alcohol but thought this latest crackdown was downright discriminatory.

"It's like they're trying to get rid of us, but that's never going to happen," she said. "I bleed pinstripes."

Security guards hoping to enforce the alcohol ban were never a match for the Creatures' creative and technical innovations.

Inebriating fluids were smuggled past security guards at the gate quite easily. Mike Donahue carved out the inside of submarine sandwiches and put beer cans inside. Another fan simply wrapped a fifth of Bacardi rum in his jacket. As he was frisked at the turnstile, he would lift his jacket up in the air, along with his rum, and no security guard would bother to check above the waist. The most common trick of all was simply to fill empty Poland Springs water bottles with the necessary potions.

If nothing else, the fans figured the alcohol ban in the bleachers was saving them a great deal of money. A beer at Yankee Stadium now cost eight dollars, the price of a single bleachers seat in the season package. The club was sacrificing tremendous revenues at its refreshment stands but apparently felt that the more "fan-friendly" atmosphere in the bleachers was attracting families and increasing gate sales. There had been fewer fights and complaints.

Nobody could argue with the effectiveness of that marketing strategy again on this night, when another long line of consumers started at the ticket sales window and snaked around the back of River Avenue. The Yankees were leading the leagues in both home and road attendance, averaging more than 47,000 in the Bronx. No other team was close. Only the Angels (41,114) and the Dodgers (40,331) were averaging more than 40,000. George Steinbrenner could not help gloating over his empire, issuing a statement thanking the fans but really patting himself on the back for putting together a winning team again. He was also sending a not-so-subtle message to Bud Selig and the other owners that the Yankees were bolstering the league and shouldn't have to pay into the revenue sharing pool.

"Two thousand four will be recorded as the year of the extraordinary Yankee fan!" Steinbrenner wrote through his personal public relations man, Howard Rubenstein. "As the team demonstrates its enormous talent and heart on the playing field, Yankee fans throughout the tri-state area are responding by coming out to the stadium in record numbers. But it's not just Yankee Stadium that is seeing capacity crowds. Our team is helping fill ballparks throughout the country when we play. This turnout is simply unprecedented and speaks to the excitement of our New York Yankee team. Who knew you could hear a Bronx accent in Seattle, Texas, or so many other ballparks?"

The Yankees' insane popularity had clearly impacted on what was once a life of few formalities in the bleachers. A few years back, lines were rare and it was a common practice to sneak in without paying, employing such tricks as counterfeit or duplicate tickets. None of that was working anymore. Just recently, guards began scanning the bar codes on the bleachers tickets as fans entered, yet another crackdown to dampen the mischievous spirits of the Creatures.

The fans came anyway. They paid; they got scanned. They could not get enough of this stuff, even if it was just the lowly displaced Colorado Rockies in town. Interleague play at Yankee Stadium annually meandered from the sublime to the inane, and clearly here was one of the more absurd matchups: the Rockies in the Bronx. There was no history in this AL–NL matchup, no allure, no star power. Colorado was a generically mediocre team with a horrid road record at sea level, where baseballs in flight were forced to meet actual molecular resistance. It was hardly worth the effort for the right-field fans to create appropriate heckles for the assortment of Colorado's journeymen right-fielders, who were standing in front of them. The most exotic thing you could say about the Rockies was that their manager, Clint Hurdle, had gone against conventional wisdom by sticking with a four-man starting rotation. This, however, did not make for a catchy taunt.

There was a missionary's argument for the Yanks to visit baseball-challenged cities like Denver, where they would be a rare diversion and a great draw. There was no logical argument, however, for bringing the Rockies to New York. This season the Yanks would host the Rockies, Padres, and Mets in interleague play. They would visit the Dodgers, Diamondbacks, and Mets. Of those six series, only the ones against the Mets and the Dodgers made any sense in the minds of Yankees fans. The Creatures didn't even like the Mets series. It was just another nervous time when the Yankees

Bald Vinny's T-shirt stand is a successful business for the Bleacher Creature. (Larry Palumbo/Coyote Magic Photography)

were expected to defend their turf against the mediocre, ambitious invaders from Queens. It was not impossible that the Yanks might some year lose four of six games to these bumblers. Baseball was a strange game, and anything could happen. Mets fans would brag big time at such a watershed event. It was not a pleasant possibility.

The Creatures were happily planning their road trip to Los Angeles and wished they could go to San Francisco to renew an old New York rivalry against the Giants. Barry Bonds versus the Yankees would have been a wonderful showcase for baseball, but it was not on the schedule. No matter. Attendance figures at the stadium were becoming ridiculously lofty, and the Rockies wouldn't ruin that. At one time it required a beautiful Sunday afternoon, Bat Day, and the Red Sox in town to assure a decent crowd. Now any team could visit the Bronx on a rainy weekday afternoon and the place would still be mostly full. A three-game series against the Texas Rangers had just drawn an average of more than 51,000 fans to the park. The regulars came, and the corporate types came, and foreign tourists to New York City suddenly believed a trip to the stadium was a must-do on any three-day itinerary. The Yankees were on target to break every one of their own attendance records.

In 1996, attendance was 2.25 million for the year, and George Steinbrenner was still threatening to move the team to Manhattan or New Jersey. Fans such as Bald Vinny and Tony Capone would fret about every rumor, constantly asking about a potential migration. Vinny, in particular, had a lot at stake with his burgeoning T-shirt business. Nobody worried about any of this anymore, because more than four million fans were likely to pay their way into Yankee Stadium this year, if you included playoff games. It wasn't just Section 39 that was packed now. The left-field bleachers were often sold out, too, although they were not even opened on this night, when 39,000 came to watch the Rockies.

The game itself was unconventional. Kevin Brown, the fragile 39-year-old ace who already had amassed a 7-1 mark, slipped off the rubber throwing a strike in the first inning and hurt his back. He stiffened up, gave up four runs in two innings, and was replaced going into the third by Tanyon Sturtze. The Yankees' middle relief held tough, the Yanks rallied, moving more than three games ahead of Boston. Still, this was quite a scare with Brown. He had two injury-wrecked seasons out of the last three. When you looked at his resume, it read like an advanced anatomy exam: hyperextended right elbow, stress fracture of the rib cage, dislocated right index finger, bruised right leg, broken right pinky finger, right Achille's tendon strain, cervical radiculopathy, severe strain of the flexor muscle of the right elbow, release of scar tissue and swelling in right elbow, and posterior medial strain of his right elbow.

Brown had suffered through all of that, and now he had vague trouble with the lower back, which defied any cold clinical terminology. Anybody with a bad back could tell you that it will put 10 years on you, and Brown was too old to give up another decade. Even after his best performances, Brown would flagellate himself for bad location or stupid pitches. He never lived up to his own standards. After this disastrous start, he was particularly flustered. He kept repeating how he wasn't pulling his own weight with this team, despite that 7-1 record. He offered to keep pitching into the third or fourth inning—"I wanted to give our bullpen a chance," he said—but Torre wisely ordered him to take a seat in the dugout. Brown would have tests for his back in the next couple of days. While he did, another key starter Mike Mussina would take himself out of a game on Friday night with a strained groin muscle. For a team that was steamrolling the competition, the Yankees were giving their fans a lot of reasons to whine and worry about the pitching in October. It was one thing to outscore the Rockies of the world and quite another to push across this many runs against the Red Sox, A's, or Astros.

Before and after the game, Bald Vinny stood his ground outside of Stan's bar on River Avenue to sell his wares, his precious $10 T-shirts. According to the agreement with the vast empire of Stan's, his shirts needed to retain a bleachers motif so they didn't overlap with Stan's wide range of souvenir shirts. When he strayed too far from that rule, like when Bald Vinny manufactured some "1918" shirts to humiliate Boston fans, he was ordered to cease and desist.

Vinny had an odd protector of sorts in undercover cop Tom. True, Tom hated the Creatures with all his Mets-loving soul, but he had a soft spot for Vinny. To be more accurate, Tom had a bald spot for Vinny. In a previous incarnation as a marketer for a razor company, Vinny had supplied Tom with an efficient head-shaving implement. It was a token of affection from one bald man to another, no bribe, but it apparently created an odd bond between the two hairless wonders.

"We take care of Vinny," Tom said, standing by the stadium.

This arrangement had helped Vinny avoid most of the usual hassles aimed at independent vendors in and around the River Avenue neighborhood. Vinny's business had not made him a millionaire, but it paid the rent on his Queens apartment and all the car payments. He had bought his own silk-screening machine in February 2003 and became an officially incorporated business in April. He did all the printing himself. His merchandise was on sale here at the stadium, but also in Baldwin, Long Island, and over the Internet, at www.RFBleachers.com.

A graduate from the University of Hartford, Vinny was one of the most active, but also one of the gentlest of the Creatures. He was a born planner and was always in the middle of the most ambitious Section 39 ventures—from the annual Central Park softball game scheduled for July 31, to the Los Angeles road trip, to the 100-ticket purchase for the upcoming game against the Mets at Shea. His delightful girlfriend of seven months, Rose, had only recently displayed the first sign of losing patience with his commitment to the Creatures. She understood why he went to all the games, to sell his T-shirts and to see his beloved Yankees. But why did he have to hang out with these guys at other times, instead of with her? Was that road trip to L.A. really necessary?

"I see her point," Vinny said.

Still, he couldn't stop himself. This was a close social set and a tough habit to break. He called last year's softball game "the best time I ever had" and intended to become thoroughly involved in the drafting of Creatures for this year's game. The draft would be held at the new Jeremy's Ale House, down the block from the old one. Vinny had already been to the new Jeremy's, even before it opened, to scout out the tavern and to see whether the lingerie décor of the old place was appropriately transferred to the new hangout. It was.

Rose was in for a rude awakening or else destined for martyrdom, because Bald Vinny was not going to change very soon.

UNTIL THE END

he Creatures quite often arrived late to their seats, but they were not supposed to leave the stadium early. It was the code of the bleachers, of Section 39, to stay in place until the final out was recorded, ignoring at all costs the hopelessness of the situation or the growing traffic outside heading north on the Major Deegan. Somewhere, deep inside these bleachers fans, there may have been lodged the secret desire to get home at a reasonable hour, to escape a one-sided game, and to manage seven hours of sleep before rising for work the next morning. But to admit such a thing would have been treason. The box seaters who perched across the right-field divide were derided mightily for their fair-weather antics and for their migrations toward the exits at the sight of a three-run deficit. Where on earth could they be hurrying to that could possibly be better than this Eden in the Bronx?

The more time spent here, the better. In the not-so-old days, before reserved seats, most of the Creatures would get to the bleachers before the steel gates were rolled up along the River Avenue entrances a couple hours before game time. This was always the best time to grab a baseball, either off a batting practice homer or from a generous outfielder strolling near the right-field wall. The odds of getting a baseball were remarkably good, especially early on when there were probably no more than 30 fans hustling for 10 to 20 batting practice homers. You just had to park yourself in a relatively isolated row and wait.

Maybe it was relatively easy to get a baseball before the game in Section 39, but it became much tougher during or after the contest—even in the bleachers. It was just too crowded; the odds were against you, especially in the bleachers where fewer fans departed before the final out. They were the truest of believers. Never was this lesson in patience more rewarded than on this

Little Mike and Tone516 celebrate a run with the legendary triple high fives as Bald Vinny's girlfriend, Rose, cheers the Yanks on. (Larry Palumbo/Coyote Magic Photography)

Sunday afternoon, when the fans who stayed together, celebrated together. It was a remarkable game, with a little bit for everyone.

First, David Wells, a Creature favorite, returned to the Bronx and pitched seven shutout innings for San Diego. Wells was adored by fans, although he was never a beloved figure in the Yankees clubhouse. Mel Stottlemyre, the patient Yankees pitching coach, couldn't bear dealing with the guy. When Wells left Game 5 of the 2003 World Series after only an inning with a sore back, he'd pushed the Yankees coaching staff past its breaking point. The rubber-armed lefty had not warned anybody of any soreness while boasting about his invincibility. Taking Wells at his word, Torre had sent Andy Pettitte ahead back to New York to prepare for Game 6, leaving the manager with only shaky Jose Contreras as an option to finish up Game 5. That 6-4 loss arguably cost the Yankees the championship. Even though Torre desperately needed a fourth starter in 2004, the Yanks offered Wells only a non-guaranteed contract, the ultimate snub for a 200-game winner. Wells instead chose San Diego, near his home but far, far away from the championship banners.

So there was still a lot of resentment on both sides, and Torre, usually a fine storyteller, would not offer a single anecdote to reporters before the game about Wells. In the bleachers, though, Wells remained a considerable hero. He and David Cone had been the only two pitchers ever to acknowledge the first-inning roll call with a tip of the hat, and Wells always went out of his way to say that the Creatures were his kind of guys. His late-night antics and his punchout in a diner only endeared him further. When Wells wrote in his own book that he was half-drunk when he pitched his perfect game for the Yanks, he sealed the love affair. He was living the ultimate Creature dream, guzzling beers and setting down opponents in order. He could do no wrong.

He was greeted this Sunday afternoon with great affection, a standing ovation. Wells required only 75 pitches to throw seven shutout innings and then left when he rubbed up a blister on his foot. He heard nothing but cheers the whole day.

"I'll probably remember this for the rest of my life," Wells said. "The fans are great, they've always been on my side. It was kind of hard to leave. But things happen. All I can do is come back and show them I can still pitch."

The Padres took what seemed a safe 2-0 lead into the ninth, except that nothing was safe anymore against the Yankees. With two out and nobody on, as some of those box seaters left and headed for the Deegan, Hideki Matsui and Kenny Lofton homered off closer Trevor Hoffman to force extra innings. San Diego scored three more in the top of the 12th inning, and surely this was the end. Again, the few remaining fans who were not sitting in the bleachers gathered their stuff and departed. By now, it appeared that half the spectators remaining were in and around Sections 37 and 39.

Such faith was well justified. The Yankees managed their league-leading 27th come-from-behind victory of the season with a classic rally. Bernie Williams walked; Derek Jeter doubled. Gary Sheffield hit a one-out single. Giambi singled. Former Yankee Jay Witasick came in for relief, and he allowed a ground-rule double by Jorge Posada to tie the score. Finally, Ruben Sierra won the game with a sacrifice fly. Game, set, match. The Creatures who stayed for this three-hour-and-47-minute game had seen it all: a fine day from old friend Wells and then two unlikely comebacks by the home team. More than 67 percent of the Yankees' victories this season had been produced by comebacks, adding to the famous mystique and aura of the pinstriped uniform.

That concept was once mocked by visiting pitcher Curt Schilling, now on the Boston Red Sox. Back in 2001, when his Arizona Diamondbacks faced the Yanks in the World Series, Schilling said that Mystique and Aura were dancers in a nightclub, not factors in a best-of-seven championship. But he soon discovered differently, when the Yankees made impossible ninth-inning, two-out comebacks in Games 4 and 5 of that series. Wells would not deny the existence of such magical pinstriped spirits.

"I've seen it plenty," Wells would say afterward. "When you're here, it's great. When it happens to you, you shake your head and say, 'It's still happening.'"

```
JUNE 27, 2004                                              (47-26)

                    1 23  456  789         R  H  E
        METS        000  000  100          1  3  0
        YANKEES     211  000  04X          8  8  1
```

```
JUNE 27, 2004                                              (48-26)

                    1 23  456  789         R  H  E
        METS        010  101  201          6  10  3
        YANKEES     600  100  40X          11  12  1
```

THE OTHER
TEAM

The sadistic baseball commissioner, Bud Selig, insisted on scheduling six Yankees–Mets games every season, causing great angst and resentment in all quarters of the New York metropolitan region, including Section 39. The games were probably good for business, because they helped sell many extra tickets at Shea and didn't hurt the sales in the Bronx. But the cost was far too great in terms of familial and neighborhood relations. The fallout was toxic: Friend versus friend… brother versus brother… Tina versus anybody with a Mets cap in the right-field bleachers.

"I forgot how much I hate these people," Tina said about Mets fans, after a Saturday victory by the Mets. "More than anybody. More than Red Sox fans. I can't take it. They make me sick."

The Yanks have a rivalry with the Mets the way a whale has a rivalry with plankton. The Mets arrived in the National League in 1962, going 40-120 that first year as the Yankees were on their way to another world championship. Although there had been unaccountable dips and surprise ascensions (most notably in 1969 and 1986, the Mets' only two championship seasons), the Yankees generally were the dominant team. This was reflected very clearly in head-to-head games. The Mets and Yankees faced each other in city charity exhibitions, in spring training exhibitions, in inter-league regular-season play, and in the 2000 World Series. And in every one of these categories, the Yankees held an edge. Going into the games this night, the Yanks were 87-56-1 overall against the Mets. After this doubleheader sweep, the Yanks would be 26-13 in interleague play against the Mets. Most importantly, the Yankees were forever 4-1 in World Series games.

"After what we did to them in 2000, nothing really matters anymore," Bald Vinny said. "They can't say anything."

October 2000, that Subway Series, would always be locked away in the collective memory vault of the Creatures. Everything had been at stake, and the Yankees did exactly what the Yankees were supposed to do. It was both a scary and heady time.

"If we win, it's the cherry on top of the sundae," Tone Capone had said at the start of that World Series. "But if we lose, what are we going to say? The Yankees will be fine, with all the championships. But everything the fans stand for will be thrown into the garbage."

It had cost $50 a pop for this moment of truth, for a ticket to the best madhouse in the Bronx, Section 39, Mets versus Yankees. You could scalp those tickets for nearly 10 times that much, which was a terrible dilemma for cash-strapped bleachers fans. A couple of the regulars, most notably Capone, had been caught and detained for scalping during another series. Usually, the cops kept these entrepreneurs in a holding cell for the length of the game, which was punishment enough. There was no TV and no radio broadcast of the game available in the cell. It was worse than being consigned to isolation.

With exactly such punishment in mind, Milton, the cowbell man, decided to keep his ticket for Game 1 of the 2000 World Series.

"This is the video game I've been playing since I was a kid, Yankees against the Mets," Milton said.

The difference was that Milton could always shut off the video game if the Mets got a big lead.

"Nostradamus said that World War III will start in New York in the year 2000," Milton said. "The first bomb drops tonight."

It was such a tense period, the Creatures had embraced allies they normally would reject. Shaky alliances were forged with several traditional enemies in order to fend off the vilest of rivals. Box-seat fans, the ones rooting for the Yankees, were suddenly treated respectfully, or at least they weren't cursed openly. Yankees fans with ties on and even with painted faces were all welcomed, reluctantly, into the temporary alliance against the Mets. If a high school marching band wanted to join in, Section 39 might have accepted its members as honorary Creatures, as well.

"We'll even cheer the guy dressed as Mr. Peanut, because he can whip Mr. Mets' butt," Sheriff Tom Brown said.

The Yanks won Game 1, 4-3, in 12 innings, and then everybody began to relax a bit and make fun of the box seaters again. The Bombers would capture the championship in Game 5 at Shea. A few of the regulars were present for that one, but the real celebration came at the victory parade, down the Canyon of Heroes. These parades that meandered through Wall Street had become old hat—this was the fourth in five years, after all—but the one in 2000 felt somewhat fresh because it involved the humiliation of half New York's baseball rooters. It would also be the last hurrah for a while.

Sheriff Tom was in a perfectly fine mood along the parade route, having spotted and retrieved some pornographic confetti before anybody else (Tom identified the stuff early, noting the material's glossy color as it sailed down from the 40th floor of a nearby building). But he strained his right shoulder and would need his strength to hoist many beers later at Jeremy's Alehouse. Luckily, Tom was a switch-drinker.

Milton somehow finagled another invitation onto the Modell's float at the victory parade. He had managed this before. He was some operator. But as he rode past City Hall, Milton found himself sitting on the wrong side of the float and couldn't clang his bell for the Creatures who were lining the parade route. Instead, a counterfeit cowbell man banged out rhythms. The Section 39ers made do with a bow from Bernie Williams and modest waves of acknowledgment from Joe Torre and Paul O'Neill.

"Now we can finally put all this Yankees–Mets nonsense in a hole and throw dirt on it," Mike Donahue had said. "We had to wait three years for this ugly prom date and now, whenever Mutt fans pipe up, we can finally just say, 'Shut up,' plain and simple. 'Move to California.' Next year, the Mets should take off the 'NY' and put a big 'L' on their caps."

The L, of course, stood for losers.

There were wagers to collect back then, from poor deluded Mets fans. Donahue's roommate was sentenced to a month of cleaning after losing his bet. Poor Sheriff Tom couldn't win, though, even after winning. On one of his wilder and drunker escapades (pre-marriage, pre-child), he had talked some women into the world's oldest bet. Then he lost their numbers because somebody—probably a Mets fan, he figured—pick-pocketed his cell phone on the subway.

"I had their telephones, their e-mail addresses… ," Sheriff Tom lamented.

That result, that series, would always be a defining New York baseball moment. But it wasn't just the 2000 Series that separated these two franchises. It was absolutely everything. The Yankees owned the pinstripes, the famous names from the past, the celebrities in the stands, the historical setting in the Bronx, and the owner who spent money like a maniac. The Mets had those silly orange and blue colors, left over from the 1964 World's Fair in Flushing Meadows. They played in dilapidated Shea out there in Queens, their stadium facing away from Manhattan. The uniforms and caps changed colors every day, blue to black to white. The grounds crew mowed the grass in weird, psychedelic patterns. The jets made too much noise taking off from neighboring LaGuardia. The sound system was tinny. The owner, Fred Wilpon, wouldn't part with the millions for Vladimir Guerrero. There weren't even any real bleachers at Shea, just a wholesome family region beyond the left-field wall called the Pepsi picnic area.

"Did you know the Pepsi picnic bleachers are on wheels, so in the seventh inning when the Mets are getting crushed they can just roll the whole section out into the parking lot?" Donahue said, starting his routine. "The Pals are about as dangerous as foam rubber. Can't wait to see them paste another wildcard sticker on the right-field wall. Their stadium is starting to look like the bumper on a Winnebago."

Donahue had many other Mets fan jokes, some about babies in garbage bins that were never quite printable. He was not alone in his disdain.

"It's like they're cartoon characters," Milton was saying. "They get all excited. They scream, 'Let's go Mets.' They're orange. They're not real."

Whenever they came to the bleachers, to the stadium, the Mets fans stuck out like crass Texas tourists in Paris. There was, for example, the man sitting alongside his 10-year-old son, whose face was painted with the Mets colors.

"Why doesn't the father just paint a birthmark on the kid's face, and maybe put some braces on him?" Donahue wondered. "That stuff won't come off without gasoline."

There was the woman with bright orange shoes. There were Mets moppets. To Yankees fans, it was a real freak show out there.

"Every year, every time they come in here for a new series, we get new Mets fans here," Chris Cartelli said. "You look at the jerseys they wear, there are no Seaver jerseys, no Dykstras. They're all black and orange. There's just no heritage there."

If this sounded harsh, Yankees fans felt their counterparts had nobody to blame but themselves. They hadn't been born Mets fans. They elected to live this way. It was a lifestyle decision. Donald Simpson was proof that this crucial distinction between Yankees and Mets fan was not determined by genetics but was rather a conscious rebellious choice. His brother, Danny, remained a rabid Mets fan. Before every season began, for more than a decade, the delusional Danny was tremendously confident that the Mets would first unseat the Braves and then defeat the Yankees in a World Series. He was an unfailing optimist. Donald remembered how at the start of the disastrous 2003 season his brother insisted the Mets were a sure thing. They had stolen a possible 20-game winner and future Hall of Famer from the Braves in Tom Glavine, had a "rejuvenated" Roberto Alomar, had a "lighter" Mo Vaughn, had enough "protection" for Mike Piazza in the batting order, and got plenty of speed on the bases with Roger Cedeno. Danny actually termed the Mets lineup "awesome." The Mets finished 34½ games behind both the Braves and the Yankees and lost all six head-to-head meetings in the regular season with the Yanks.

"What I try to tell my brother, Danny, every year," Donald said, "is that the Mutts simply suffer from one very simple yet complex disease that seems to afflict only Mets fans and their beloved team. It's a disease called, 'No-matter-what-you-do-to-try-to-make-your-team-competitive-it-will-always-be-second-class-as-long-as-the-Yanks-are-in-New York-itis.'"

The Mets had started the 2004 season hopefully, as their new general manager Jim Duquette promised to get younger. By June, they were sagging below .500 and had replaced their batting coach—a sure sign of desperation for any club. But now they were feeling their oats again, marginally contending for first in a truly terrible division. Richard Hidalgo, acquired by the Mets from Houston for peanuts, had turned back into a fearsome hitter. The Florida Marlins and Philadelphia Phillies were real disappointments so far, allowing the Mets to hang in there, within three games or so, far longer than they deserved.

This is not to say the Mets lacked their share of devout followers. A poll by the *Daily News* showed that readers were nearly split in their loyalties between the Yanks and Mets. Romanticists from the Brooklyn Dodgers era began to dredge up the old "U.S. Steel" argument again—that it was more fun to root for a team that lost its share of games rather than for a monotonous juggernaut like the Yankees. This might have made more sense if the Mets were a more exciting team, but they couldn't hit for power, and Howe was not exactly turning them into the Go-Go White Sox of the late 1950s. The Mets were weak on fundamentals. All you had to do was watch Piazza throw the ball from his new ill-fitted first base position, and it was enough to make you pine for his catching assignments. So it was hard for Mets backers to assume the higher moral ground against fans of the far more functional Yankees.

Some of the Creatures reveled in the Mets' misfortunes. Tina, as she said, hated Mets fans like she hated nobody else. She looked truly pained and outraged whenever she saw one in the bleachers. Others, such as X-Pac, tended to take pity on the Mets.

"Those poor souls cross-town," he said. "They have the anti-Midas touch where everything they do crumples and falls apart.

Art Howe isn't fully adjusted to the all-consuming cesspool of Flushing known as Shea."

It was easy to say that Yankees fans shouldn't kick the Mets when they were down. But the Mets were almost always down and sooner or later required a kicking.

Bald Vinny much preferred invading Shea for these games, rather than defending the home turf against intruders in the Bronx. He had a stockpile of 100 tickets, ordered before the season, for the upcoming three-game set at Shea.

"It's not at all like with the Yankees," he said. "You can order as many tickets as you want. They just want to get rid of their seats."

The Yankees fans told you they didn't like these games against the Mets, even as they filled every seat in the stands. The managers grumped that the series was the worst sort of irrelevant distraction, even as they choreographed each game as if it were Game 7 of the World Series. Torre knew that George Steinbrenner was watching very closely and would not abide losing five of six. Art Howe understood that six games against the Yankees (three in the Bronx, three in Queens a week later) were not likely to help his team's divisional standing.

The first game on Friday was rained out. The Mets won the scheduled second game on Saturday 9-3. It was, Marc Chalpin said, "not much different than an ordinary June loss." Some of the Bleacher Creatures watched the game at Jeremy's, the relocated South Street Seaport hangout. A few Mets fans got in their face during the loss, but the debate didn't last long.

"Congratulations," Chalpin told them. "You're now 13-24 against us."

Now there was this doubleheader on Sunday and more angst. The result, a sweep by the Yanks, was more a relief than anything. For a few days, at least, there would be no boasting by Mets fans, who were growing more precocious by the minute.

"This is nothing like previous years in my opinion," Chalpin said. "It isn't supercharged at all. The buzz isn't there. This series has lost its significance. There's more intensity but not much more. After 2000, it just isn't as important. This series means just slightly more than any normal series. We have nothing to gain from beating the Mets. It lowers the magic number, that's about it. It counts in the standings. They could win every game for five years, and that would put them at about .500 in the all-time series, and even if they did that, we still beat them in the Series."

This was a fairly typical opinion of Section 39ers, who preferred never to face the Mets again in their lifetime. Back in 2000, those Series games were far too close, and there were uncomfortable plot twists. The strangest one was probably the Roger Clemens–Piazza confrontation. Clemens had beaned Piazza during the season for no apparent reason, and then Piazza broke his bat on a Clemens fastball in the World Series. Clemens picked up a bat shard and hurled it in the general direction of Piazza, who was trying to run to first and suddenly was forced to avert some flying wood.

Piazza had done nothing to Clemens except take his pitch to the noggin. The throwing of the bat shard was a completely irrational act but turned Clemens into a temporary redneck folk hero in the bleachers. Until then, he had just been an ex-Red Sox star, a mercenary tethering his wagon to pinstripes in search of a championship legacy. The Piazza feud changed all that, at least for some. A photo of Piazza appeared on the Bleacher Creatures' then-new website, with a bull's-eye around his head. That was when the rivalry was at its most heated, obviously, when a run here or there might have toppled the existing world order.

The doubleheader victory on this Sunday was not so special, but it provided another chapter in the oppression of one New York team against the other. The whale had eaten more plankton. The first game also offered a notable plot twist: Jose Contreras was pitching in front of his family for the first time. Contreras had been chronically and perhaps clinically depressed since fleeing Cuba in October 2002 without his wife, Miriam, and two daughters, Nalan and Naylenis. The $32 million contract was not enough. He was finally reunited with them the previous week after they were smuggled out of Havana. Contreras looked a lot more at ease now and more confident, as his family watched from a luxury box. He was able to control his forkball, his favorite pitch, in crucial situations such as in the fifth inning, with two outs and the bases loaded, when he threw one to the Mets' Kaz Matsui. If he had walked Matsui, a run would have scored, and Piazza might have come to the plate with the bases loaded. At least for one game, Contreras seemed to be a new man, and his family joined him afterward at the press conference.

It was a heartwarming story, but basically the fans in Section 39 understood this wasn't a big game in October against Boston and were just happy to get a decent performance out of the guy. The Yankees' starting rotation remained ragged. In the second game of the doubleheader, Mike Mussina struggled and gave up a couple of homers to Hidalgo. This was all disturbing to the stalwart Yankees fans in the crowd of 55,387, the largest of the season at the stadium. It hinted at problems to come, although nobody could complain about a doubleheader sweep or the 51/2 game lead over the Red Sox.

Boston was coming to town for a three-game set, and the feeling was the Yankees could finish them off earlier than usual. Unlike these games with the Mets, the Creatures found a visit from the Red Sox welcome and strangely reassuring. There was a score to settle from those first two series, when the Yanks were discombobulated and the chants from Section 39 weren't honed yet. Unlike these pesky Mets fans, Boston backers rarely lived next door or in the room across the hall. They were safely housed somewhere up the New England Thruway and were correctly forced to suffer great psychodramas in the Bronx each and every autumn.

	1	2	3	4	5	6	7	8	9	10	11	12	13	R	H	E
RED SOX	0	0	0	0	0	2	1	0	0	0	0	0	1	4	10	0
YANKEES	0	2	0	0	1	0	0	0	0	0	0	0	2	5	11	2

REVENGE EXACTED

People around the Yankees often said there were 162 seasons every year with this team, that every game became a psychodrama of overblown proportion because the Yanks were expected to win every one of them. A more accurate multiple might be about three, because every Yankees victory seemed about as important as a three-game winning streak for a normal baseball team; every loss as dire as a three-game skid. Whenever the Yankees really dropped three straight games (nine straight by Bronx math), the panicky reaction by George Steinbrenner, by New York papers (even the staid *New York Times!*), and the fans of New York was greatly amusing. Demands for trades or straight cash acquisitions abounded. Individual Yankees were fingered for terrible scoldings. Such responsibility and pressure came naturally with a payroll approaching $200 million. But even within that overwrought and overly expensive framework, some games were viewed as more special than others. And this one, an epic struggle against the Red Sox, became one of the best baseball affairs of the season.

Many of the regulars hadn't been at the game, it turned out, because they lacked tickets. As noted, those season packages didn't always include the most popular games. But some of the fans had gathered at Jeremy's Alehouse to watch together, and others simply turned on their televisions at home. They were still buzzing about the drama, which had more surliness and plot twists than any current Bleacher Creature feud.

Pedro Martinez, the man who wrestled last October with Don Zimmer and was everybody's favorite villain at the stadium, struck Gary Sheffield with a pitch in the first inning. Sheffield had annoyed Martinez by stepping out of the box a couple of times before key pitches. There was an angry confrontation between the two men, and Pedro was jeered. But the Creatures were nothing if not discerning fans, at least when they were watching the game more objectively on television. Bad Mouth Larry, a knowledgeable student of the game, decided that Sheffield deserved the beaning, because "he stepped out twice, and the last one was very blatant. Pedro had the right to do what he did, in my mind." The game meandered into extra innings, and then Derek Jeter dived into the stands in the 12th inning, sacrificing his body while chasing and catching a shallow fly ball hit by Trot Nixon. Jeter left the game bloodied as a great hero. The Creatures compared Jeter giddily to Nomar Garciaparra, who had missed the key game with another minor injury. Eventually, John Flaherty singled in the winning run in the 13th inning. After a three-game sweep by the Yanks, the Red Sox were now 8½ games behind, nine in the loss column.

Revenge had been exacted for those sloppy April contests, for Boston's sweep in the Bronx. The results appeared to deal an early death blow to Boston's hopes of winning the AL East. Usually the Red Sox made it to August before fading. This time they hadn't even reached that legendary halfway point, the Fourth of July. Even more delicious for Yankees fans: If the playoffs began on this day, the Red Sox would not have qualified as a wildcard team. The A's were starting to make some noise in the AL West, behind Texas, and it was remotely possible that Boston would become the odd team out.

That long-shot scenario amused the Creatures no end, as they gloated over their victory. The next morning's *Daily News* featured the biggest headline as simply, "Wow!" and there were only baseball players, Yankees, celebrating all over the back page. The Yanks were on a five-game winning streak, and it felt like 15.

	1	2	3	4	5	6	7	8	9	R	H	E
TIGERS	0	3	1	0	3	3	0	0	0	10	13	0
YANKEES	0	2	1	0	0	0	5	0	0	8	10	1

TROUBLE AT THE STADIUM

Terence Williams found out about the mess when he reported to work in the morning, about four hours before the Wednesday afternoon game. Williams, the security supervisor for the bleachers, had taken one lousy night off, and all hell had broken loose Tuesday in and around Section 39. It was no coincidence. Terence was the most effective of behavioral scientists, a virtual virtuoso in the way he conducted the Creatures in his seating sections. He knew when to lead, when to bend, and when to stand firm. There were implicit deals brokered between Terence and the Creatures, unwritten but fully understood. Vulgarity was a relative term, and it was tolerated during some games but not during others. By Terence's reckoning, Yankees games carried a rating, like movies. Some were PG, some were R, and then a few night games against the Red Sox were rated XXX.

"On Friday nights, I'll disappear for a while, let them sing a song or two," Terence said. "Just as long as they give me the weekend. You don't want your kids listening to that stuff."

Misbehaving was something of a tradition in the bleachers, although it generally took the form of a controlled burn. The mischief was varied, from innovative and witty to simply nasty. The Creatures liked to think the rules were their own in Section 39, although certain compromises had been made along the way.

"Here, we're just people with nothing in common, banding together against a common enemy—the world," Paul Kaplan once said, when he wasn't rolling along the aisles during the seventh-inning stretch.

Kaplan had this theory that the Creatures required an outside enemy to protect them from themselves. And there were times, when the games and the competition were dull, the intramural

Terence Williams is in charge of keeping the peace in Section 39. (Larry Palumbo/Coyote Magic Photography)

fighting could get ugly, like when Tone Capone took a swing at Mike Donahue over a fight about who was fatter.

"Without a decent team to root against," Kaplan said, "we start cannibalizing each other."

There were plenty of potential targets, including the infra-structure of Yankee Stadium. One Creature had been sentenced to community service for pulling out a seat from the stadium and trying to take it home, after the Yankees won the World Series in 1996. Sheriff Tom Brown's brother, Dave, once heckled his own niece, who was performing before a game with a high school marching band, until she was left in tears. Female visitors to Section 39 unfamiliar to the core group might be heckled with the chant, "Ice cold bimbos." A few of them had been reduced to tears over the seasons, too.

When the Padres played the Yankees in the one-sided 1998 series, a group of mellow San Diego fans somehow found their way into the bleachers, a big mistake. By the time they returned to Southern California for Game 3, they were shell-shocked. During interviews with local San Diego TV stations, they related horror stories of New York fans.

"I was just holding up my banner, and then the next thing I knew it was on fire," one woman told a field reporter after arriving at the airport.

Sometimes the fans would lack hard targets and aim at softer ones, perhaps the vendors. Back in the days when there was alcohol allowed in the bleachers, one of the women might scream, "Hey, beer man!" After he came clambering up 12 rows of seats, she would slyly finish her request, "Hey beer man—where's the soda man?"

Before he got a regular job that kept him from far too many games and a few altercations, Tone Capone created a set of very specific battle guidelines aimed at visiting Boston fans. First, he began with the standard "Welcome to Hell!" chant. Second, a "1918" taunt, with special emphasis on the first syllables of each number. Third, a slight spillage of liquid, preferably beer, on the backside of a Boston fan.

"Then we see," Capone would say. "Either they take it or there's a confrontation."

Although this sort of action was clearly provocative, at least Capone was consistent in his methodology. That was more than you could say for the enforcement techniques used by police stationed around the stadium. On some days, they were generous, friendly, and helpful. On others, they could be just plain mean, chasing down "unofficial" vendors, locking them up for selling knockoffs, and sniffing out every open beer can on top of the parking garage.

"The same police officer who's chatting you up on Monday is giving you a ticket for public drinking on Tuesday," Sheriff Tom lamented. "You don't know what to expect."

There was more consistency inside the stadium in the bleachers, which was Terence's domain. But on Tuesday night against the Tigers, without Terence in attendance, the scene had been volatile. The Creatures were out in force, and the Yankees were losing big to the Tigers. On paper, this did not appear to be a flashpoint matchup. Tensions should have cooled after the series with the Mets was done, and the emotional baggage had been stowed away again in New York's mixed-fan households. It had not been an easy week. Bald Vinny led about 100 Creatures to Shea Stadium in Queens, and these heartiest of Yankees fans were mocked mightily while the upstart Mets swept all three games. It was yet another example of a post-Red Sox letdown for the Yanks that was very common. Recently, whenever the Yanks beat Boston in a series, they would follow their victories with losses to a lesser team. And whenever they lost to Boston, they were awakened by the defeats and cobbled together a winning streak.

At the disastrous three-game set in Shea, Junior nearly got himself tossed when he took exception to getting searched not once, but twice, by security. One Mets fan was wearing a helmet with a dust broom attached, and the taunts of "sweep" were unending. The Creatures behaved themselves, swallowed their medicine, and expected a hospitable homecoming at Yankee

Stadium. They sought the tranquility that comes with 40,000 good friends gathered together in a familiar old building.

But then on Tuesday against Detroit there was an exchange of beanballs on the field, and the Yankees' rotation continued to sputter. In the stands, it grew worse. One guy in Section 37 was tossed from the bleachers for screaming obscenities. He somehow popped up again waving down at the cops from the adjacent upper deck. Milton, the cowbell man, moved to his usual position in the third inning, standing by the rails over the portal that divides Sections 37 and 39. This had been his perch, his precious band-stand, for eight years running. Milton climbed up on the first rail, so that the rest of the bleachers fans could see him while he banged out his rhythms. But for some reason, on this otherwise ordinary night, a policewoman took exception to Milton's cowbell ringing. She told him to move away from the rails and that he was block-ing the view of everybody else. Milton refused, of course, explain-ing reasonably that he was practically licensed to do this and that the cowbell was a tradition dating back to Ali Ramirez. Milton was in no mood to be hassled. He had just been through a lot of other nonsense with his cowbell in other ballparks. In Los Angeles, on the Creatures' road trip, he was prohibited from bringing his cow-bell into the stadium because it was deemed a potential weapon. Milton then managed to knock his bell at Shea, but that just made him the target of more abuse by triumphant Mets fans.

Milton stood his ground in the Bronx. The problem would have ended right there, except that Terence wasn't around to arbi-trate. Instead, his replacement backed the cop and told Milton to move immediately. Again, Milton refused. An intermediary guard told him he could stay in the stands if he just didn't bang his cow-bell. Such conditions were unacceptable. Milton left. There would be no rallying clangs and no Yankees rallies. The sight of Milton's semi-forced departure was so infuriating and the game itself was so offensive, the regulars felt the need to leave in protest or to be ejected. Suzy cursed, loudly. Bad Mouth Larry announced he would get himself thrown out as well. He cursed (nobody curses as effectively as Larry, hence the nickname) and left in a huff. As

Milton, the cowbell man, and fellow Bleacher Creatures get the crowd to make some noise. (Larry Palumbo/Coyote Magic Photography)

the score grew more one-sided against the home team, the Creatures felt they really had nothing to lose. A half-dozen of them were escorted out, and many more simply left on their own.

It was quite the sight. The most loyal fans in New York were deserting the ballpark, as if they were spectators at Dodger Stadium trying to beat the freeway traffic. Bald Vinny went out early to River Avenue to sell T-shirts. Junior left in the eighth.

"They were wrong," Terence said about how the security team had cracked down on the Creatures and created a bitter scene. "I'll talk to them."

Tina wasn't there that night either and insisted later none of these things would have happened if she'd been around to negotiate with the cops and calm Milton down.

"Won't happen again," she promised.

It was a lousy night all around. The mother of a loyal bleachers fan had died. A bunch of his friends went to Jeremy's to offer sympathy and condolences.

That was Tuesday, but now Terence was in charge again on Wednesday, and there were thousands of kids all over the ballpark for an afternoon game. This was a harmless enough scene. It almost felt like an exhibition game, although it was still an important test for the Yanks. They had dropped four of their last five, and they were starting yet another stopgap pitcher, Brad Halsey.

Junior was in charge of leading the roll call today. Bald Vinny was taking an extremely rare day off. It was strange to see the sidewalk in front of Stan's bar empty of his wares. The Creatures guessed that his girlfriend Rose finally read him the riot act after all his traipsing across the nation. Vinny handpicked Junior to start the roll call, and so Junior took off from his job with food preparation at a Queens hospital. Junior was treating these sacred responsibilities seriously. He would start very carefully with Bernie Williams, as always, then move around the outfield and infield. The bleachers were definitely shorthanded today. Milton was at work. Tina was missing, along with most of the regulars. As school-age kids made their way up the cement steps in the bleachers, a few stopped to read the plaque on Ali's seat. For many, this was their first time in Section 39. They would require some educating.

The game was disturbing from the start. Halsey was rocked for seven runs in four and one-third innings, further proof of the team's fragile starting rotation. This was becoming an obsessive topic of conversation and a worrisome theme for the season. The bullpen was getting overworked, too. The Yanks fell behind 10-3 and then rallied in the five-run seventh that included a three-run homer by Alex Rodriguez. They fell short, though. Even the mighty Yanks hadn't come back from a seven-run deficit in 17 years, and today would be no different.

Orlando Hernandez, "El Duque," would be returning after the All-Star break after an extended stint at Triple-A Columbus. But he was 38 and hadn't pitched in the majors for two years.

Nobody knew what to expect. For now there was no real ace, and the Yankees were still forced to beat teams by outscoring them. Some fans boasted about the fact that the Yanks led the league in comeback victories, 31, but Statman would tell you that was a troublesome statement about the team's starters. The Yankees were not the Yankees anymore, at least not the same model franchise that captured four pennants in five seasons from 1996 to 2000.

They were hitting the tar out of the ball, no argument there. They had the best record in baseball, true enough, at 51-31, so it was difficult to whine too loudly. The Yanks led the majors in homers with 125, were third in runs scored with 455, were second with walks at 365, and were third in on-base percentage at .355. But at the same time the earned-run average of their starters was now 4.98, flirting with that embarrassing 5.00 mark, ranking 23rd among the 30 teams. They were suffering through a six-game streak in which five starters had yielded 30 runs in just 32 innings. During that stretch, not one of them had lasted seven innings, and the Yanks had given up nine runs or more in those games on four occasions. Considering Steinbrenner's investment in Kevin Brown (out with some weird intestinal parasite that had also struck Jason Giambi), Mike Mussina, Javier Vazquez, and Jose Contreras, these were humbling numbers. The Yankees were still paying a heavy price for the escape of their three veterans, Wells, Clemens, and Pettitte. The club was feverishly trying to work out a deal for Randy Johnson before the trade deadline at the end of the month, but there weren't many Yankees prospects left to trade to Arizona. The other available starters on the market, such as Kris Benson from Pittsburgh, did nothing to excite anybody.

The games were thrilling enough, better than ever, filled with late-inning plot twists. No lead was safe on either side of the linescore. The Section 39 regulars were getting their money's worth. Then again, they always did.

```
JULY 21, 2004                                    (59-34)

              1 23  456  789        R   H   E
BLUE JAYS     0 02  001  000        3   11  0
YANKEES       0 54  010  000        10  15  0
```

LOVE AND MONEY

Romances and family obligations continued to interfere with Section 39 duties, eating into the Bleacher Creatures' rooting time. Sheriff Tom, once the stalwart of the bleachers, was only showing up on Fridays with his wife, Dana, and kid, Emma, who was starting to learn Yankees names.

And then there was Milton, the cowbell man. Milton had his own family, and the Creatures understood that. But he was now appearing at only about half of the games and didn't always have the best excuses. The worst example of such confused loyalties occurred when the Yankees were playing the Red Sox on April 24, a disheartening one-run defeat, and when Milton was seen on TV the same day at the NFL draft, ringing his cowbell at the Jets' selections from inside Madison Square Garden. Milton had a way of finding the TV camera. There were many harrumphs over that episode. Talk was growing about possibly acquiring a backup cowbell man as discontent spread. The cowbell was a sacred ritual instrument. It was also a great recruiting tool. Fans from all over the park would hear the cowbell and migrate to the fun, deserting their posh box seats for the funky Latin rhythms. Now, there were only the roll calls and the chants without the musical accompaniment.

Mike Donahue had none of these distractions at the moment. His social life was not exactly hopping, he had to admit. A couple of years earlier, he'd been dating a woman, Danielle, who bugged him in August about attending a friend's wedding in October. This, of course, was an impossible request. The playoff schedule was still unknown. For all Donahue knew, he would commit to the wedding, and then the Yankees might suddenly be playing against the Red Sox at the stadium in the American League Championship Series. Donahue didn't know what to do at the time, so he called Bad Mouth Larry to get some advice for the lovelorn. And to this day, Donahue cites Larry as the ultimate sage on romantic matters. Larry's counsel? Simple. Don't argue with her, because it's not going to matter.

"If she's bugging you now about going to a wedding in October," Larry counseled Donahue, "then you're not going to be going out with her for long. She's not the one."

She wasn't. Donahue liked Danielle enough, but they couldn't stop fighting about his schedule and a million other things. One of my columns focused on their relationship, quoting Donahue as saying Danielle had broken up with him 17 times.

Danielle saw the article and screamed at Donahue, "I've only broken up with you twice."

Sheriff Tom, his wife, and daughter enjoy an evening in the bleachers. (Larry Palumbo/Coyote Magic Photography)

Then she broke up with him a third time, for good. So that was it for Donahue, at least for a while. He was working the bar at O'Brien's Pub in New Rochelle and was looking forward to the wet T-shirt contest on Friday. He was a confirmed bachelor and attended almost every game he desired.

Then there was Bald Vinny, who was living a midsummer night's dream. Vinny Milano seemed to have it all. He'd met Rose Stanzione over the Internet last year. She thought it was cute when he grumped that no women were answering his ad, so she did. The Queens couple hit it off immediately. And by now Rose, clearly a saint, was coming to more than half of the home games in the Bronx, and she often was keeping Vinny company at his T-shirt stand before and afterward. On this particular evening, and most games, Vinny's concession stand was located no more than 10 feet away from a beggar laid out on the sidewalk before his homemade sign, "Why lie? I need a beer." A second beggar introduced himself to Vinny as a mental patient and said that only a dousing with cold water could bring him out of his dementia. A couple of fans gave him a dollar. This was hardly a romantic meeting place, but Rose was totally unaffected by the scene. She showed up with sandwiches for Vinny. She even paid for them.

"He's done a good job of incorporating me," Rose said. "And he promised me that the road trips were on the downswing."

They weren't, of course. Section 39 and related activities were still very integral to Vinny's social life. He'd gone out west with the Creatures, and he had organized the 100-ticket outing to Shea, and he would be heading soon to Toronto. He was also excited about the big softball tournament set for Central Park in another 10 days, which had begun with a controversial draft at Jeremy's. (Sheriff Tom was annoyed he'd been selected very late, Donahue confided.) Basically, Vinny was booked solid through October. But Rose was hopelessly brainwashed. Nobody could believe this woman's sweet, accommodating nature. Undeterred by the chaos, Rose was scouring Section 39 for more bachelors, hoping to make matches for other friends. Maybe.

"I want to set them up," she said about the men of the bleachers. "But I've seen them too much and know them too well."

Tina came to the game with a friend but didn't look well at all and finally said she didn't feel right. It took a lot for her to admit that. Her stomach was aching. She was grimacing. As with any cancer survivor, there was always the fear that her pain was connected somehow to that brutal disease. Tina didn't think so.

"It's probably my ulcer," she said.

She would go to a doctor next week, she said, for another checkup. Tina wasn't sleeping much and wasn't eating well. Her personal and professional life was in constant flux. She often depended on the kindness of friends to get her through another day, and sometimes those hopeful plans would fall through. She was still hoping to throw out the first ball at the Creatures' Central Park softball game, though.

By now it was quite clear the Yankees were going to be playing in October again. Their brief July slump was a distant memory. Rumors about Randy Johnson had been heating up as the trade deadline approached, and the topic of conversation among the fans was whether signing Johnson was necessary or even the right thing to do.

Although they will deny it until the end, Yankees fans were somewhat defensive about the team's spending sprees. It grew tiresome arguing that a big payroll alone didn't assure championships and that it merely guaranteed contention.

The topic of predatory capitalism was an uncomfortable one that struck close to home. There were deals being made everywhere around Yankee Stadium every single day, and some of them were even brokered by the Creatures. A couple of weeks earlier, Bald Vinny agreed to include the name of a Yankees employee in the ritual Bleacher Creature roll call of players during the first inning. In return, the employee delivered an autographed A-Rod baseball to Vinny from his personal stash. The deal was done, sealed with a chant.

Morality was a relative thing in the Bronx, where you followed the money through the turnstile and down the rabbit hole. George

Steinbrenner's pursuit of Johnson would be a gambit of the grandest scale, yet it could be seen in basically the same terms as Vinny's roll-call transaction. The Yankees were dangling money (plus marginal prospects) at the Diamondbacks, hoping to obtain a service in exchange. Big bucks for the Big Unit. Was it outrageous, avaricious, evil? Or was it standard company business with an interlocking N-Y?

"The Yankees, for as far back as I remember, had people shaking their heads, even before free agency," Joe Torre philosophized in the dugout before the Yanks out-spent and whomped Toronto 10-3. "This is the same situation. It's just the rules have changed. You work for this club; it's the same 12 months a year."

Despite their gaudy record, the Yankees still were short an ace for October. Mike Mussina could barely touch his shoulder with his hand, and Kevin Brown was last seen fighting nasty parasites and giving up five hits in four innings to Pawtucket (a Red Sox farm team!). Even in victory this particular night against Toronto, Javier Vazquez didn't look great. He yielded three runs and nine hits in six innings. Vazquez lost his rhythm at times and walked in a run with a 5-0 lead.

"We'll be fine in two weeks," Torre figured.

The Yanks looked fine right now, outscoring opponents on most nights. It might be fun to see if they could simply crush opponents in October, the way that Anaheim did in 2002. But Torre was fighting a nagging suspicion that these 2004 Yankees were built very much like the Cardinals in the National League— both constructed for the six months that preceded October, the only month that counted.

The moral imperative to acquire talent, the Yankees' Manifest Destiny, seemed just as important sometimes to George Steinbrenner and Brian Cashman as the signings themselves. Several recent expensive additions felt particularly gluttonous, even to Yankees fans—not because of the money but because of heartfelt loyalties to core players. Jason Giambi replaced beloved Tino Martinez. Kenny Lofton came aboard to nudge Bernie

Williams into the role of part-time center-fielder. The arrival of Alex Rodriguez meant the departure of buoyant Alfonso Soriano.

In the case of Randy Johnson, this would not be a problem. The team's starting rotation was currently on its second or third generation of transient mercenaries. These pitchers marched through as if visiting a shopping mall. Some were likable (David Cone), some prickly (Mussina and Brown), some overzealous (Roger Clemens), some wacky (David Wells), and some just plain disappointing (Jose Contreras). Once Andy Pettitte left, there was no homegrown talent available to discard or humiliate. If Johnson came to the Bronx, he would only bump Contreras, or someone of his nomadic ilk. There was nothing unsettling about that.

The broader issue, however, remained open for debate: Were the Yankees and their closing-in-on $200 million payroll responsible for the decline and fall of the Selig Empire? Everybody was entitled to an opinion on the matter, and his view was often determined by his rooting interest. Cashman's old line that the Yankees were not built by money and that they were instead the product of their own farm system and well-researched trades was now a laughable notion. The whole Yankees economy was spinning, accelerating to levels unmatched in any other ballpark. TV revenues dwarfed those of other teams. Everything was for sale, including the scoreboards and the right-field wall, where Japanese characters incongruously spelled out yet another company name, Yomiuri, to the great embarrassment of the right-fielder, Hideki Matsui.

The fans, unmindful of their increasingly commercial environs, still came like crazy. The Yanks had another ridiculous crowd, 53,031 for a Wednesday night game against the last-place Blue Jays. The next four games against Toronto and Baltimore were all but sold out. So much money, so much pressure. If this were the end of baseball civilization as we knew it, then it was a lucrative apocalypse.

Even the players were aware of the growing crowds attending the games and were talking to each other about the phenomenon.

"You can't help but notice," Bernie Williams said. "We're winning, there are a lot of stars on our team, and they're selling good baseball."

The Yankees were certainly playing well, although several players were far from peak form. Giambi was a shadow of himself. He fretted that his disease was something much worse than parasites.

"These baby steps won't cut it," he said impatiently, of his recovery.

Giambi even muttered the C-word, cancer, to reporters, although tests would prove negative. Derek Jeter was nursing a slightly displaced fracture on his hand after getting hit by a pitch for the 91st time in his career. Jeter wouldn't back off the plate, and he was resisting the idea of wearing protective gear. He missed this one game, aiming instead for the Red Sox series in Boston. Williams, meanwhile, was still struggling at the plate, and he walked around the clubhouse under the weight of a giant ice pack on his shoulder. He had gone into the manager's office to assure Torre he would start hitting soon. Out of loyalty and confidence, Torre kept Bernie in the lineup almost every day in center field or as the designated hitter.

There was always a cure for what ailed this team. When one Yankee slumped, another stepped up. Somehow the Yankees just kept winning, the crowds kept storming the box office, and the Creatures would have to endure the nuisance of all these new faces in the right-field bleachers.

AUGUST 2

THE DOG DAYS

A ll the varied events that shape a season in the bleachers
do not necessarily take place in and around Section 39.
By mid- to late summer, the standings were less interesting, and the games melted like gum on the sidewalk
into a sticky amalgam of Bronx heat and humidity. The Yankees
were now so far ahead of the Red Sox, while the Mets lagged so far
behind the Braves in that other outer-borough race, there was not
much amusement left to be found around town in the six-month
dance leading to the playoffs. It was at this time of year, the dog
days of agate type in the daily newspaper, when the Creatures were
at their creative best while spinning tales or planning events. Left
to their own designs, bleachers fans were quite good at entertain-
ing themselves.

The second annual softball tournament in Central Park had
been a great sensation, well attended and extremely competitive. It
was also a study in the Creatures' organizational skills. G.B. Steve
Krauss did the paperwork and got a field permit many months in
advance. Players from the inaugural game were given first crack at
reserving spots in the lineup. The rosters were expanded from 11
to 12, and a fourth team was added to meet the growing demand.
Four captains were selected (Midget Mike and Tone Capone were
politely but firmly informed they would have their turn in 2005).

Sheriff Tom, picked extremely low in the draft, exacted his
revenge with an MVP performance in Game 1 and then by winning the championship on Steve's team (although Tom went zero
for three in the title game). Many controversies erupted, enough
to fill the month of August with point and counterpoint.
Everybody agreed that the highlight arrived when Bad Mouth
Larry unleashed his famous temper at Phil, who was catching for
the opposing team.

It all happened so quickly. Bad Mouth Larry was called out at home plate in the sixth inning after an elaborate base-running drama. With runners on second and third and two out, The Dever fielded a grounder and inexplicably decided to get Larry in a rundown rather than throw to first for the easy out. Marc Chalpin botched the throw to third. Christina, the third baseman, retrieved the ball and threw it home as Larry steamed to the plate. Phil didn't do a great job of blocking the plate, but Larry was called out anyway. Larry had to be restrained, while a surprisingly serious brawl erupted among the teams. Larry was a captain, and his players refused to take the field after the call, setting off a 10-minute delay with darkness looming.

Marc Chalpin lobbied the ump to get Larry's team on the field or to announce a forfeit. Tensions mounted.

"I wanted to win that game badly, and a lot of people that worked for so long to make it happen felt the same way, including Larry," Chalpin said.

Eventually, Larry's team took the field and then came back in the top of the seventh with a huge rally on Larry's run-tying triple. His team leapt from the bench and began celebrations.

"Mets-like celebrations," Chalpin fumed.

Even Larry was annoyed with his teammates' behavior, because the game wasn't over yet. Sure enough, Chalpin's team came back to win when The Dever nailed a game-winning single in the best softball game to date.

Many photos were taken, and a video camera caught the action. These developments were particularly topical, because the Yankees themselves had recently become embroiled in their own brawl with the Red Sox up in Boston. A total of eight players from the Yanks and Boston were disciplined by league official Bob Watson. Alex Rodriguez and Jason Varitek both received four-game suspensions plus fines for their roles as instigators. It was extremely doubtful, however, that Bad Mouth Larry would face a similar suspension from softball organizers. Larry had every intention of appearing at the third annual game in 2005. Meanwhile he was reveling in the fuss. His meandering postgame rationalization

A wild skirmish broke out during the 2004 Bleacher Creature Softball Challenge in Central Park because of a controversial call at home plate. Jack Frost holds back the captain of the MFers, Bad Mouth Larry, as Larry tries to get Phil. (Anthony Griek)

for the tantrum was refreshingly honest compared to sterile, well-practiced quotes from real major leaguers.

"Phil had some set of balls, knowing that I was safe, to use a bullshit defense that I shouldn't get home because I hadn't been at third base [when the throw went off-line]," Larry fumed. "I wasn't at third because of The Dever's interference. Phil's defense was bullshit, and I lost it. What's funny is, I forgot how that play happened. Nobody even remembers the rundown I got out of that created that play. I think Marc threw it away... I love running the bases."

A special two-DVD set of highlights was culled from the tournament. Stills from the DVD were sent off to a professional batting instructor for some analysis of the sorry swings that had been on such public display in Central Park. Already, there was talk about next year's draft and how the athletic stock of some Creatures had risen or fallen dramatically. Walkman John was quite the softball stud, with uncanny skills in all categories: hitting, fielding, throwing, and running. John would be a first-round pick next year for sure. But Milton, the cowbell man, who had captained the championship team just a year earlier, had been a disappointment, and he would suffer accordingly.

"It was the team I got picked on, it wasn't my first choice," Milton grumped. "They even picked a girl in front of me."

Meanwhile, the wet T-shirt contest at O'Brien's bar in New Rochelle, Mike Donahue's workplace, had been another successful diversion for several of the fans. And at that same bar, Donahue came upon a tale that demonstrated again the special symbiotic relationship between the Bleacher Creatures and Yankees players. Donahue was drinking with another Creature, Chris Cartelli, and with a Yankees ballboy, who happened to be in the area. The ballboy, plied with alcohol and prodded with questions, eventually enlightened Donahue and Cartelli about the fate of the fans' famous rubber chicken.

The chicken had been a regular guest in the bleachers from 1998 to 2000, at home and road games, at Creature parties, and at other social gatherings. There were photos still passed around from those days that included the rubber chicken in the foreground, background, or simply atop somebody's head. But one day during the 2000 season, while the chicken had been tossed around the bleachers during a home run celebration, Cartelli had carelessly flung the precious icon onto the outfield grass. The ballboy, their current drinking buddy, had retrieved the chicken with one of the player's mitts, and the Creatures had waved goodbye to the sacred poultry as its head and neck bobbed around furiously, all the way to the dugout.

"A rubber chicken in a Yankees mitt isn't something you see every day," Donahue said.

At the time, Donahue had begged one of the security guards to retrieve the chicken. Donahue had fibbed a bit, claiming that the regulars had been completely innocent. It had been a perfect stranger who'd tossed the chicken onto the field, Donahue said with a straight face. But his plaintive appeal had been nixed, and it had appeared the chicken's three-season run at the ballpark was complete.

But over drinks at O'Brien's, Donahue and Cartelli were pleased to discover the chicken had not gone quietly into the night. The ballboy explained that the rubber novelty item was never returned to the Creatures for good reason. It had been adopted by the Yankees players inside the clubhouse, who would hold a secret ballot each week to determine the "Dick of the Week." The player who won this unwanted honor would then have the privilege of displaying the chicken inside his locker. The Yankees were so dedicated to this practice that they commissioned "D-O-W" T-shirts, which were more or less forced upon the comrade elected to the position.

Just knowing that the Creatures had contributed in this small way to a roguish culture inside the clubhouse was a rush of adrenaline, at just the right time—during the dog days. The pennant race was becoming a joke, yet another laugh at the expense of Boston fans everywhere. The only question remained whether the Red Sox (now without Nomar Garciaparra, who had been dispatched to the Cubs) would get their act together long enough to qualify as the wildcard team. The trade deadline was past, too, and with it any sense of anticipation. After all the fuss, the Yankees hadn't managed a trade for Randy Johnson. Instead, they sent Jose Contreras to the White Sox for 32-year-old Esteban Loaiza, plus the requisite cash to ease the burden of Contreras's contract. John Olerud was about to sign also to begin duties as first baseman in place of Giambi, who was still ailing with what the club called simply, defensively, a benign tumor.

Remember that heartfelt reunion story involving Contreras and his family? The Creatures had never really bought into it, and now Contreras and his legend were somebody else's business. The bleachers fans no longer cared about it in the slightest, if they ever did. This was why the fans rarely invested their emotions and loyalty in Yankees pitchers, with the exception of Mariano Rivera. The hurlers came, they won a few games, they left by way of trade or free agency, and they were forgotten quickly enough.

Loaiza was probably an upgrade from Contreras, most agreed, although there was no telling for certain. In 2003, Loaiza had been stupendous, going 21-9 with a 2.90 ERA. This season, he was 9-5 with a more human 4.86 earned run average. Loaiza had been in two straight All-Star Games, but he was no Randy Johnson. Mussina was expected back soon enough, so the Yankees' rotation figured to be Mussina, Vazquez, Brown, Loaiza, and then either "El Duque" or Lieber. This seemed a reasonable combination and a staff filled to the brim with No. 2 starters, lacking only that one killer ace.

Mostly the bleachers fans were glad to be done with Contreras, who had been erratic much of the time and consistently horrible in games against the Red Sox. Nobody believed he could be counted on in October. The response in Section 39 to Contreras's departure was nearly unanimous: good riddance. One fan said he was glad Contreras was out of New York, with or without a raft in the Caribbean. Another wondered sarcastically if Contreras would choose to go into the Hall of Fame as a Yankee rather than as a member of the Chicago White Sox.

There was realistic skepticism about Loaiza, too. The most commonly held opinion was that general manager Brian Cashman had traded one bullpen pitcher in the playoffs for another bullpen pitcher in the playoffs. Marc Chalpin thought this was a truly unremarkable transaction.

"I don't think Loaiza is all that good," Chalpin decided. "He had one good year. Great. But unfortunately, this isn't that year. The benefit is that it gets a lousy pitcher off our team in favor of a pitcher who isn't that great. The general neutral view is that Contreras actually has better stuff. But I guess it's safe to say it will never happen for him in New York, so they might as well go with another pitcher."

It was hard to get too excited about Loaiza, about first place, or about anything right now. The Yankees were winning more than their share. But the veteran bleachers fan understood that the long season had its own rhythms and demanded patient pacing. August was hardly the time to become too enthralled with anything, except vacation. The fans kept coming in droves to the stadium, anyway, most of them first-timers and strangers to the core group. The remote left-field bleachers were open for business at every game, a sure sign of another enormous crowd. The Yankees were now so successful at drawing sellout or near-sellout audiences, the club issued a public warning to fans that they should take mass transportation and arrive early at the ballpark.

"The Yankees established an all-time single-season franchise attendance record in 2003, drawing a total of 3,465,585 fans to Yankee Stadium during the regular season," the club declared. "Through 51 home dates this season, the Yankees are averaging nearly 50,000 fans per game and are on pace to break the franchise mark for highest attendance."

The fans arrived like ants to a picnic. The Yankees were nine games ahead of Boston now, sleepwalking to the division pennant. To the Creatures, this was no big deal. It was August, it was very hot, and the playoffs were still too far away.

	1 2 3	4 5 6	7 8 9	R	H	E
ANGELS	0 1 0	0 0 0	2 0 2	5	13	1
YANKEES	0 0 0	0 0 0	0 0 0	0	5	1

A DARK ALOHA

It was Hawaiian shirt night in Section 39, and most of the Creatures arrived in their wildest getups, hoping to enhance what appeared on the schedule to be just another game. Bald Vinny and his girlfriend, Rose, wore the same patterned shirts because, as Vinny explained, "We're cute." There were many groans over this sight. And then, at 8:55 p.m., with nearly three innings left in an otherwise lackluster contest, the power went out in the Bronx.

Bob Sheppard had just introduced pitcher C.J. Nitkowski, utilizing his usual golden tones. And that would be Sheppard's last name of the night. This was a local blackout, nothing like the city-wide disasters of 1965, 1977, or 2003. The lights stayed on, so the game itself was unaffected, but all the layers of modern-day junk and static melted away like magic. There was no longer an electronic scoreboard telling fans when to cheer. There were no psychedelic advertisements dancing along the facades. The fans, players, and officials on the field were forced to keep track of the score and the game stats on their own, with clickers and longhand notations.

"What's the count?" became the most common question of the night in the stands.

Statman could always provide the answer, of course.

"It's nice not to have all the 'boings' screeching around here," Midget Mike decided, reveling in the silence of it all.

You didn't realize how polluted the baseball games had become with invasive modern trappings until these frills suddenly disappeared, mercifully, from the scene. Yankee Stadium, despite its classy reputation and deep historical roots, was one of the worst offenders when it came to artificial pomp and electronic contamination. The place could be loud, crass, and headache inducing. On top of the usual faux military displays ordered before games by

Milton, the cowbell man; Tina Lewis; and Donald Simpson take in the action in their best Hawaiian shirts for Hawaiian shirt night. (Larry Palumbo/Coyote Magic Photography)

Walkman John checks the official scoring on the play. Was it a hit or an error? (Larry Palumbo/Coyote Magic Photography)

George Steinbrenner, there were these awful commercial intrusions and mindless scoreboard games between innings, pumped up to a volume that discouraged, even prevented, normal conversation. There were quizzes, advertisements, Yankee-ographies, and heavy-metal intros for the batters. There were warnings about throwing stuff on the field, and there were instructions on the scoreboard to clap, to get loud, or to get excited over a single or a base on balls. Sometimes, the scoreboard just displayed the single word, "NOISE."

"I hate all that stuff," Midget Mike said. "Drives me crazy."

A lot of things drove Midget Mike crazy, but in this regard he was in the majority. Left to their own means in these final three innings, without a single electronic instruction, the 53,530 fans did quite well. Instead of singing "Take Me Out to the Ball Game," "God Bless America," or "Cotton Eyed Joe" during what is usually the interminable seventh-inning break, they started the simple chant, "Let's Go Yankees." Then somebody in the box seats began the dreaded Wave, which died when it reached the Creatures again. The Wave would never survive the bleachers, as long as there was a Creature left alive to kill it.

The game itself did not meet the lofty standards set by the Hawaiian shirts or the blackout. The Yanks lost in desultory fashion. The Red Sox, once 10½ games behind, were starting to creep up on the Yankees, who were playing without much spunk. Amazingly, Orlando Hernandez had become the ace of the staff. "El Duque" was barely in the picture during spring training. Back then, he was running laps and trying to get into some sort of pitching shape, while nobody paid him any attention. Now, with Mike Mussina and Kevin Brown battling injuries, Hernandez was suddenly the most consistent starter on an inconsistent staff.

Again this night, Torre had to go to a reliever earlier than he wanted. And when he tried to call the bullpen to get Paul Quantrill warmed up for the ninth, Torre couldn't get through. The mini-power outtage had wrecked the bullpen phones, just as it had knocked out the lights in the clubhouse. Torre was set to send an old-fashioned messenger down to the bullpen, but then somebody out there finally noticed and told Quantrill to get up for some tossing. It was 1940 all over again, a welcome relief from technology. You could almost see Joe DiMaggio in center field, chasing down a fly. And if Joe had looked up in the bleachers, he would have seen that Bald Vinny and Rose were wearing the same Hawaiian shirts, the way he and Marilyn surely did…

```
AUGUST 31, 2004                                    (81-50)

                    1 2 3   4 5 6   7 8 9      R  H  E
INDIANS             3 3 3   0 6 1   0 0 6     22 22  1
YANKEES             0 0 0   0 0 0   0 0 0      0  5  0
```

THE HITS
KEPT
COMING

E very baseball season requires its darkness before the dawn. And here was a prolonged midnight, pitch black and without explanation. In the right-field bleachers, after a while, nobody knew whether to laugh or whether to commit suicide. Most fans simply chose to leave early, rather than wallowing in self-pity. In the long-fabled history of the Yankees, they had never been humiliated so badly. They'd lost twice by 18 runs in the 1920s, and they'd been shut out 15-0 twice by the White Sox, once in 1907 and again in 1950. But this was different, very real, and immediate. This rout wasn't culled from some history book. It was more than some faded black-and-white photograph. The proud Bombers, the modern version, were getting demolished in clear sight of Sections 37, 39, and 41, and all regions of the stadium. They were being humbled by lowly Cleveland, a hopeless franchise with smiley racist cartoons on its caps.

The Yanks fell way out of this game early, down by nine after just three innings and down by 15 after five. By the fourth inning, there was a whole lot of jeering going on. Fans had many reasons to be upset, beginning with the notion that Javier Vazquez, ostensibly the team's best pitcher, had sabotaged the evening with another woeful start. Joe Torre more or less guaranteed a great performance from Vazquez, a bit of wishful thinking that did not survive 15 minutes of pounding. Vazquez was just terrible, and the parade of relievers who followed was no better. Esteban Loaiza, who'd proven to be a disastrous acquisition and had been demoted from the rotation, gave up six runs in a final inning of relief. The Yankees were trying to dump Loaiza practically from the day they traded for him; that's how bad he was. Brian Cashman, the general manager, had not done enough homework on the guy, whose reputation for flightiness preceded him by several seasons.

Midget Mike is always ready to grump about something. (Larry Palumbo/Coyote Magic Photography)

Torre left Loaiza in there on the mound against Cleveland, down by double digits, as punishment. All this took place in plain view of 51,777 fans and George Steinbrenner, who happened to be at the game watching in horror from the owner's box. Steinbrenner would refuse comment, later issuing another cliché-ridden statement from his public relations man, Howard Rubenstein. You could only imagine what Steinbrenner was really thinking while watching his team, with a payroll that had grown to nearly $200 million, lose by 22 runs (an average deficit of about 1.1 runs per $10 million spent).

Of all the Creatures in Section 39, only Midget Mike seemed to take perverse pleasure in the proceedings. When things turned ugly, he led the chants, "We want 20." Cleveland obliged him and then some. Midget Mike was a mailman, who always pointed out that the other mailman in the bleachers, Mike March, was just an express mailman. Midget Mike was the world's biggest curmudgeon in other words, and he was actually having a good time, as everybody around him reeled from the spectacle. Midget Mike and several other bleachers fans got into a screaming fight with one specific fan, telling him to sit down, then telling him to stand up, and eventually inciting the poor fellow to act in such a profane fashion as to get himself ejected from the park. The guy was so upset about what happened, he hung outside the stadium later in search of the offending bleachers fans. Nothing came of it, just as nothing had come of any Yankees rally.

Regardless of the score, all fans who left the game before the final out were fair game for mockery in the eyes of Midget Mike. For those who considered this kind of game a litmus test for blind dedication, 22-0 became a good argument that Sections 37 and 41 were becoming more fanatic than Section 39. You looked around the bleachers, and the place was a ghost town except for 37 and 41.

"The core group in 39 is slowly losing its commitment," Bald Vinny decided. "Section 41 is a comer. There's new blood there."

He noted Vinny sold T-shirts to all the right-field bleachers, sections, and he qualified as a neutral observer of sorts. There was some new blood in Section 39, too, personified by the brash young newcomer Tone 516, who screamed with the best of them, right up there with Bad Mouth Larry.

No matter where the fans sat, they were clearly distraught over such a one-sided defeat. The Red Sox were now 3½ games behind, having trimmed a full seven games off the once bulging lead. The Red Sox, those sneaky opportunists, had chosen to make their stealth move during the dog days of the season, when nobody was paying much attention. Boston was on a 15-1 tear, and the competition didn't seem to matter. The Red Sox just kept winning on the East or West Coast. A broad-vision fan might argue that the Yanks still held an eight-game lead in any potential wildcard race against the AL West and were therefore a virtual lock for the play-offs. The last two champions, Anaheim and Florida, had both been wildcard clubs, proving that a team suffered no real disadvantage in the postseason by qualifying in this fashion. But the fans in the bleachers didn't want to entertain such back-door entries into October. They looked no further than the suddenly claustrophobic AL East race, and a Yankees pitching rotation that seemed badly flawed in comparison to the ones in Boston or Oakland.

"Maybe they can beat Minnesota," Midget Mike said. "Maybe."

Midget Mike was being negative again. But after a game like this one, he spoke for most of the bleachers.

	1 2 3	4 5 6	7 8 9	R	H	E
INDIANS	0 0 0	0 0 0	0 0 1	1	8	1
YANKEES	1 5 1	1 0 0	0 1 X	9	11	0

RIGHT
WING IN
RIGHT
FIELD

As summer made its final turn toward the playoffs and as the No. 4 train rattled overhead, bad vibes were palpable in the sooty air around River Avenue. The recent stint of Yankees mediocrity had taken its toll, even beyond the uncomfortably tight standings. Faith had been shaken in this team. Fans were distancing themselves a bit from their earlier hopes and projections. It suddenly felt as if Yankee Stadium wasn't the sole center of the baseball universe anymore and that there were games being played out there in Boston and other places that mattered just as much, if not more. By the standards of most baseball teams, the Yankees were still winning plenty of games and doing great business. But enough fans were missing this Thursday, leading up to the Labor Day weekend, that bleachers sales windows were open and tickets were available to all comers.

Outside the stadium, standing with his buddies, undercover cop Tom looked very happy, which was never a good thing.

"Amazing," Tom said, about how the Red Sox had trimmed eight games from the Yankee lead in just 19 days.

The Yanks were making everybody nervous, except Tom. Tempers were even shorter than the 2½ game edge in the AL East. The Republican convention was in town at Madison Square Garden, meaning that traffic was snarled, protesters were being netted by the thousands, and some of the Creatures were caught up in intramural political arguments, just like the rest of the nation. It seemed that half the website, www.section39.com, had been swallowed up by a polarized forum on Bush versus Kerry, which had very little to do with looming playoff battles like Schilling versus Mussina. The arguments were posted on the site in a category called, "The Angry Political Thread," and the screeds were at least as angry as they were political.

Some of it had become too personal, like the online war between Bald Vinny's girlfriend, Rose, and several conservatives. Sheriff Tom was one of them. Sheriff Tom was making fewer appearances in the bleachers because of family commitments. He had been a big part of four championships, though, and carried a lot of clout. Newbies in Sections 37, 39, and 41 could learn a lot from Tom, whether or not they agreed with his politics. He had been there from the beginning of this dynastic era and was able to describe the unique characteristics of each title season.

"Nineteen ninety-six was totally unexpected," Tom said, getting started. "We had the run of the bleachers to ourselves. The crew was getting bigger; we were starting to do road trips. We couldn't get enough of each other. In 1998, we were starting to become a little more cynical. It was such a strong year for the Yankees; we started to figure we'd make the playoffs every year. Guys were making wedding plans in February, so they wouldn't conflict with the World Series in October.

"Nineteen ninety-nine was more run of the mill. I was going to 50, 60 games a year, and it was getting hard to remember all of them. But the emotions were still pretty high. The year 2000, that was like a fantasy. We'd already won three championships, and we were beginning to wonder, 'How can we top this?' And then all of a sudden, we get to beat the Mets in the World Series."

By his own estimates, Tom had been to about 600 Yankees games but only a handful in 2004. He was still a prolific poster on the website, however. He was a fine tale spinner and a first-rate blogger. He was also a staunch Bush guy, while Rose was a Kerry backer. The two of them became locked in an elongated website battle.

"The whole thing makes me uncomfortable," said Vinny, who preferred to stay out of such disputes.

Vinny was considering a chat with Tom about this, hoping to calm the waters a bit. He'd tried to talk to Rose about stopping, to no avail.

"There are more than 200 pages already to the political thread, and it's all the same thing, over and over," Vinny said. "I've told her to ignore it, but she can't stop."

Rose insisted that she could handle the addiction and that she even forgave Tom his excesses.

"Inside, he's a softie," she said, and Rose certainly was right about that.

Sheriff Tom willingly admitted that he got carried away sometimes with his political diatribes. Like many newspaper columnists, he was angrier and edgier when he wrote than when he spoke.

"I look at what I type sometimes and say, 'I can't believe I said that,'" Tom said. "There are factions, and it gets ugly. Sometimes your whole day is shot from that stuff. You think it'll end after the elections, but it won't. Somebody will say something like, 'Now look what we have to put up with,' and it will start all over. Red Sox fans must be laughing, thinking our empire is tottering from the inside."

The global politics of baseball fans, of sports fans in any stadium, was a fascinating topic. There was a great deal of mob mentality involved, regardless of the city, and the loudest members of the crowd generally exuded testosterone, a decidedly patriotic and militaristic hormone. Any man or woman unwilling to stand or to doff his cap for the national anthem was sure to face some vocal consequence. Salutes to the military, flyovers, and mini-May Day parades were treated with great respect. Veterans, understandably, led the flag waving. The bleachers had their share of soldiers, like Bald Ray's nephew and "41," a veteran of the Gulf War. There were limits, though, to such positive responses. Vice presidents and mayors were traditionally jeered in most ballparks, particularly in the Northeast. Mayor Giuliani, the self-appointed president of the Yankees fan club, became an exception after 9/11. Giuliani transcended his office to become a symbol of resilience, at least in the minds of baseball fans. Patriotism trumped big-city cynicism, and he was cheered regularly. But when vice president Dick

Cheney visited Yankee Stadium, he received a prolonged Bronx jeer. It was Cheney's own fault, for making his presence known.

In Section 39 and around the bleachers, it was common for flags to be unfurled and for hands to be held over hearts whenever "The Star-Spangled Banner" played. Few people publicly grumped about the seventh-inning stretch routine, the "God Bless America" extravaganza, that stretched to more than seven minutes during the playoffs. There was evidence of more dissent on the website, but it usually didn't carry the day.

"I'm very conservative, and to me it seems more of the people in the bleachers are liberal," Tom said. "We have a lot of artsy city people. But the Republicans are so virulent we kind of drown them out. It's easy to shut them down."

The two political sides out there could usually agree on baseball matters, if nothing else. Everybody concurred, for example, that the Mets were a pathetic bunch once again, growing more hopeless by the day. There was some satisfaction in the ongoing collapse at Shea, if only because Yankees fans had endured unbearable teasing during the three-game sweep in Queens two months earlier. Now the Mets, like water, were finding their own level, and it was an extremely low one. Art Howe was clearly a lame duck, and it was becoming possible that the Mets could finish in last place after all that false optimism and bravado from their fans.

The Creatures also were near unanimity on another topic: The Yankees needed some good starts from their pitching staff in a hurry. They got one on this day, from Jon Lieber, who was at his sinker-balling best. He got 12 ground ball outs in seven shutout innings. Rodriguez hit a three-run shot in the second inning. Lieber and "El Duque" were now steadying the rotation, and the hope was that Mussina's sore elbow would heal and he could be the third reliable starter going into the playoffs. After that, it would be a crapshoot, just like the November election.

THE
PERFECT
STORM

It was billed as an old-fashioned holiday doubleheader, two games against the Tampa Bay Devil Rays beginning at 1 p.m., and in theory it sounded just wonderful. What better way to spend Labor Day than two games for the price of one? This would be a single admission throwback, not one of those day-night rip-offs. Six clean, crisp hours of Yankees baseball stretched out before the Creatures like the world's biggest chocolate fudge sundae. And of course, it was way too good to be true.

It just so happened that Hurricane Frances was churning slowly through Florida, causing $40 billion worth of damage and creating significant travel problems for the Devil Rays. The storm was no great surprise, and Major League Baseball gave the team the option of leaving Florida early for the Yankees series. But the Tampa Bay players understandably balked at the notion of leaving their homes and their families behind in the path of what was at that time a Category 4 hurricane.

"You take care of your family first and you do your job second," Lou Piniella, the Tampa Bay manager, would say. "That's the American principle, and if it's not, it should be."

So the D-Rays waited out the storm, and waited and waited. On Monday morning, the skies cleared, but bridges were still closed and the roads were still flooded. The D-Rays required about five hours to reach Tampa International Airport, where their charter flight awaited. They weren't even in the air until 3 p.m. and didn't land at LaGuardia until 5:25. The Devil Rays' bus finally pulled up to the stadium at 6:05, and by then most fans were numb from their day-long ordeal. A crowd of about 30,000 stuck around through all this, from an original paid attendance of 44,422.

Israeli Joe gets a little passionate about a Yankees game, leading to an ejection from the bleachers. (Larry Palumbo/Coyote Magic Photography)

"People are pissed," Bald Vinny reported from his T-shirt stand, when asked about the mood of the crowd in early afternoon. "Some of these people have been here since 10 a.m."

The Yankees had known on Sunday that the Devil Rays weren't going to make the 1 p.m. start and pushed the first pitch back to 3 p.m. But many fans didn't see or hear that late announcement and began showing up in the morning. The Yanks opened the gates to the bleachers at about 11 a.m., and many over-anxious fans poured inside for what would turn into a considerable wait, well beyond any rain delay in club history. After a couple hours, the fans were given the unique option of leaving and coming back into the stadium later with their ticket stubs, if and when a ball game started. You had to give George Steinbrenner a pass on this one. The Yanks made periodic announcements updating fans about the status of the games and even offered the spectators free hot dogs and Cokes while they waited. Steinbrenner would become furious with the Devil Rays.

"All they had to do was tell us they're not coming," he said.

He was angrier still with Major League Baseball officials Bud Selig and Bob DuPuy. He insisted that MLB officials had told the Yankees that the Devil Rays were trying to get to New York, when they weren't. A day later, DuPuy apologized to the fans for any inconvenience.

Free hot dogs aside, the cancellation of the day game was a terrible disappointment for families heading to the stadium for perhaps their only summer visit. But for more adaptable and veteran fans, the long delay presented a perfect opportunity to gather together atop a parking garage for a barbecue. Just past the McDonald's and up two flights of stairs to the roof, you could spend time and share some food with the bleachers upstarts from the parallel universe of Section 37. Here was fresh blood—a younger, hungrier crowd. These were more than Creature wannabes. They were Creatures in waiting, the next generation. Slowly, surely, Section 37 was becoming a real threat to the fame and glory that was Section 39, making inroads into the rooting consciousness of the bleachers.

"We don't care about them; they care about us," Israeli Joe said, about Section 39. "Like Iraq was a threat to the U.S., we're a threat to 39."

Israeli Joe said he wasn't Jewish, although he had spent six months going to school in Israel. He went by several monikers, including Brooklyn Joe and Metallica Joe, and he had rebuilt his life around the social scene in Section 37. His tale was the most ironic of all: Israeli Joe had been helped to sobriety by his pals in the bleachers. Many fans in Section 39 had been led in the other direction over the years, but here was a wholesome story from the other side of the aisle, from the Bizarro Bleachers.

"When I was boozing, the people in Section 39 were my best friends," Israeli Joe said. "But now that I'm sober, they hardly want to know me. They're all about partying."

Israeli Joe had found friendship and a real family in the Section 37 seating chart. By sheer random chance, his season ticket was one seat over from Connecticut Joe's season seat. The two Joes became fast friends, each aiding the other through the worst personal crises. And then Israeli Joe was practically adopted by a couple, the Polizzottis from Long Island, who were also sitting next to him. He called them Mom and Dad now. It was all so nurturing, you wondered if the wholesomeness would ever end.

Milton gives a stellar performance on the cowbell for Section 39. (Larry Palumbo/Coyote Magic Photography)

"Way less feuds here; none of the high school stuff going on," Connecticut Joe said, about life in 37 compared to 39. "When we start arguing about politics or anything, we stop ourselves. On the message board, wherever, we don't let it happen. We're about friends hanging out."

The group's roster was well stocked and well rounded. Section 37 had its equivalents for Section 39 and could match the section almost piece for piece, fanatic for fanatic. Statman was a stand in for Walkman John. Norma had been around as long as Tina. Cuban Monica was every bit a passionate liberal as Rose. Nature Boy, a Ric Flair impersonator, could scream right up there with Stone Cold, a Steve Austin mimic. Old Man Sam, a Section 39 defector, couldn't quite trump Old Man Jimmy in years or experience, but he was promising. And Section 37 had a top future prospect, Emerson, a nine-year-old who knew all the chants and all the moves.

"Emerson is the future," Connecticut Joe said. "And we're the new breed."

Section 37 people were generally good natured and hopelessly positive. But whenever Section 39 was brought up, an edge entered the conversation. Big Ken said he had a fight with a 39er the other day, and Little Rob said he could take no more of Milton, the cowbell man. Little Rob thought it was a bit ridiculous that Milton was making fewer and fewer appearances, now only banging his cowbells on Friday nights. He also thought Milton's recent performances were halfhearted.

"I'm throwing out a steel-cage challenge to Milton," said Little Rob, who wasn't so little. "We'll hang the cowbell up there, and both go for it."

Poor Milton had become something of a target of abuse from a wide variety of fans and for a wider variety of reasons. The top complaint was simply that he hadn't been around often enough. Whenever he wasn't there, the bleachers lacked any semblance of a musical presence. Nobody was going to usurp Milton's domain, unless it was done by official proclamation, meaning Tina. But there was a movement afoot to begin considering a cowbell replacement. Milton remained undeterred. If you called his cell phone, Milton's outgoing voice message still called himself, "The greatest Yankees fan of all time."

Maybe that was an exaggeration, but Milton deserved the benefit of the doubt, for his many years of cowbell-banging service. This wasn't as simple as knocking mallet on metal. The cowbell man needed to take the temperature of the crowd and to react to game situations with the proper pace and rhythms. Milton had been there with his cowbells for some of the great rallies of the recent Yankees dynasty, from Games 4 and 5 against Arizona in the 2001 World Series to that classic ninth-inning comeback against the Red Sox in Game 7 of the American League Championship Series in 2003—Boone's homer off Wakefield. And although Milton couldn't take credit for those offensive explosions, his bell had cut through the background roar of the crowd and given the noise a musical backbone. That counted for something.

Milton and the Yankees were first joined at the hip during his teenage years. He was a 15-year-old Brooklyn student at John Jay High School in Manhattan, when he first discovered the bleachers. He was unusually well behaved in school one day, and the teacher offered two prizes to the best students. Take your pick, she told Milton and a girl: a ticket to a Yankees game or a Walkman.

"I thought I was pulling one over on the girl, taking the Yankees ticket. Then I looked at the ticket, and it was three dollars [this was 1984], and the girl got a $30 Walkman."

Milton went to the stadium anyway, sat in the left-field bleachers, and came to a startling realization: At these prices, he could go to every Yankees game for the rest of his life. He merely required five dollars—three dollars for the ticket, one dollar for some cookies, and one dollar for the subway back to Brooklyn. (He jumped the turnstiles on the way there for a free ride but couldn't do it on the way back because there were always cops around the stadium).

"I got there early for batting practice; I saw the attention Tina got," Milton said. "She was intriguing. She was holding seats for all these people."

He hung around nearby Section 39 and slowly became a member of the group. When Ali Ramirez passed on in 1996, Tina asked Milton if he would take over the cowbell responsibilities.

"At first I said no, it was an overwhelming responsibility," Milton said. "I didn't know if I could handle it. But I took it on, and I didn't know it would turn out the way it did, such a big thing. Once the championships came, that added something to the whole aura."

The first few seasons, Milton attended virtually every game and established himself as a musical force, a dedicated replacement for Ali. If his technique was not quite up to Ali's standards, then that was an impossible yardstick. Milton was enthusiastic, and he was available—more than could be said for most. When the Yankees won four championships in five seasons, Milton became something of a local celebrity on television and in the newspapers. He was the pied piper of the bleachers, the cowbell siren from Section 39.

But nothing stays the same, and Milton had tons of responsibilities now. He had a wife, Emily, who was wonderful and who cooked and cleaned and made Milton feel like the king of his Brooklyn apartment.

"Old-school Puerto Rican," he said of Emily. "I'm a very lucky man."

He had three kids, ranging in age from two to 12. Milton was coaching his son, Eric, in Little League. He worked from 9 a.m. to 5 p.m. in Times Square as a technician in the unfortunately named shop, Met Photo, scanning and reproducing pictures.

"How do you go to games if you work? It's difficult not seeing your kids until 1 a.m."

The feuds and the changing faces in Section 39 also troubled Milton.

"It's not the same," Milton said. "A lot of the guys are younger, they're spoiled, and they forget about why they're out there. They don't respect what's going on out there. They think about the cow-bell as a gimmick. A lot of them wouldn't be sitting out there if the Yankees weren't winning. They're criticizing me, and I'm a sensi-tive person. They're booing the bell, and that turns me off from doing it. The Yankees have won so much; you don't get the same juice anymore. When they're playing Tampa Bay, you ask yourself, 'Do I have to go?'"

Sometimes he didn't go. And there was the thought in the back of his mind that maybe he should step aside. He resisted such a drastic measure. Emily told her husband, correctly, that he didn't really want to retire and that he still had too many friends in the bleachers and enough passion for his position. Besides, Milton couldn't imagine who would take his place. So he accepted the teasing, which was sometimes well deserved. He admitted proud-ly that he missed that Red Sox game in order to bang his cowbell on national television at the NFL draft.

"I'm not just a Yankees fan. I'm a huge Knicks, Jets, Rangers fan," Milton said. "And I was pumped about the guy they picked."

As further proof of his Zelig-like omnipresence, Milton some-how popped up in the background video at the Republican con-vention, holding an American flag just as George Bush walked to the podium. And Milton announced ahead of time that he would miss the next Friday night Red Sox game later in the month, so that he could participate in a John Madden PlayStation contest.

"For $50,000!" Milton said.

You could understand the cynicism in Sections 37, 39, and 41 regarding Milton's busy schedule.

The game that Milton missed this night was another example of the remarkable resurgence of "El Duque." It was now hard to remember when Hernandez wasn't part of the rotation, although it was as recently as June. He was 7-0 since the All-Star break, and the Yanks were 10-1 in games in which he started. He was absolutely essential, because the other knuckleheads on the staff were making a terrible mess of things. The worst example of this was Kevin Brown, who had broken his non-throwing hand punching a clubhouse wall in frustration a few days earlier. Some of the bleachers fans appreciated such commitment. It reminded them of Paul O'Neill's bouts with the water cooler. At least Brown cared, they said. Others wished that the starter had thought this through a little more.

"He could have thrown a chair or hit Loaiza," Cuban Monica suggested.

Instead, after smashing the hard wall, Brown required surgery and the insertion of pins (inspiring the *Daily News* headline, "Pinhead"). Now the threat loomed of a Loaiza start and a recall of Brad Halsey, the Triple-A hurler who suffered significant hammering earlier in the season. If nothing else, Brown had taken some of the headline heat off Jason Giambi, whose mystery ailment had been identified as a benign tumor on his pituitary gland.

There were those in the media who believed Giambi had kept this information secret because he was concerned it might raise eyebrows regarding his connections with BALCO, the Bay Area lab known for producing designer steroids. There were all these not-so-pleasant subplots and the interminable wait for a game. But then, when it finally started, Hernandez pitched another gem to preserve the 2½ game lead over Boston, a team that never seemed to lose anymore. Eventually "El Duque" was ejected by the home plate umpire, Rob Drake, for arguing balls and strikes in the seventh inning. By then he had staked the Yanks to a 5-2 lead. His ERA was now 2.62, ridiculously low. Hernandez suddenly had emerged as one of the top two or three stars on the team, which wasn't all that hard to do. There wasn't a single Yankees hitter in the lineup batting .300. Not one Yank was leading any of the chief offensive categories—batting, home runs, RBIs, stolen bases, slugging percentage, on-base percentage, runs scored, hits, walks, doubles, triples, or total bases. And in the pitching category, only the relievers were anywhere among the league leaders. (Rivera had 46 saves, and Quantrill had appeared in 75 of the Yankees' 137 games.)

So the Yankees won a game, although they picked up nothing on the Red Sox. That postponed first game of the doubleheader against Tampa Bay continued to cause headaches for everyone. First, it was pushed back two days, as part of another doubleheader. But both those games were postponed when the remnants of tropical storm Frances made its way up the coast. Steinbrenner was growing more furious by the moment as his home schedule, his revenue-making machine unraveled. Meanwhile, Selig was angry at Steinbrenner for insinuations that Major League Baseball had messed up the whole affair.

None of this could spoil Section 37's barbecue. Fans there passed around shrimp, veggies, and hamburgers and beer for hours without a trace of impatience. Although it had not quite been Blue Lou's Opening Day spread, the feast was impressive. These occasions had started small, with a portable grill and a few friends. They had grown into something far more ambitious. Section 37 was becoming a force as a party host.

"Section 37? They're a breath of fresh air," Milton said, graciously. "They remind me of the old bleachers."

Tina showed up at the affair and hugged a few of these fresh-faced Creatures. She was friends with all of them, an ambassador for Section 39. She just had a checkup with a doctor. She was doing well in the most important matter. Her blood count was fine. Her cancer was still in remission. She was stressed out though, and her blood pressure was way too high. Her personal life, from job to living situation, remained unsettled, and it was doing her health no good. But she delivered a book from Mary Higgins Clark.

Higgins Clark was the aunt of one of the Creatures, Chris Higgins, another example of two degrees of separation in the bleachers. Everybody was connected to everybody out there, whether it was to a famous author or to Alex Rodriguez, by way of Luis Castillo, the clubhouse attendant.

```
SEPTEMBER 17, 2004                              (92-55)

                    123  456  789      R  H  E
RED SOX             001  000  002      3  6  0
YANKEES             000  110  000      2  4  0
```

THOSE
DREADED
SOX

Yet another alleged Armageddon arrived, another three-game series with the Red Sox, and everybody on both sides of the New York/New England border was busily pretending that these games were of extraordinary importance. In reality, both these teams were surely headed for the playoffs, and it was difficult to figure out whether winning the American League East division would be in any way advantageous over qualifying for the playoffs as the wildcard team. The Yanks couldn't possibly know whether it would be easier to face Minnesota or Oakland (or even streaking Anaheim, for that matter) in a short first-round division series. The Twins and A's owned the best earned run averages in the American League (the Twins were at 4.03 and the A's at 4.13, while the Yanks were a distant sixth in the AL at 4.70). Minnesota had Cy Young candidate Johan Santana, while the A's owned a deeper, more experienced rotation. Anaheim had the strongest lineup. It also wasn't clear yet which Central or Western team would have the better record, and therefore it was impossible to predetermine matchups. No matter, though. The Red Sox fans streamed down from Boston on Route 95, driving four hours south to meet the remnants of Hurricane Ivan, the latest storm to play havoc with the Yankees' schedule, which was still a makeshift mess from Tropical Storm Frances.

Outside Yankee Stadium before the game, the usual mix of red and blue that comes with this rivalry was on parade along the sidewalks of River Avenue. Red Sox jerseys and caps paraded past Bald Vinny's T-shirt stand. As they did, Vinny couldn't resist screaming at the Nomar Garciaparra shirt wearers that their clothing line was a bit dated, since Garciaparra was now with that other cursed team, the Chicago Cubs.

For sheer quantity, the Red Sox attire on display couldn't come close to matching the Yankees stuff, and it wasn't only that way in the Bronx. Just as the Yankees held a one-sided edge on the field in this rivalry, the franchise maintained a huge marketing advantage. Yankees caps, and that interlocking N-Y logo, were an international symbol of the city and of dynastic power. If you looked closely enough, those trademark letters popped up everywhere, in the oddest places. There was a photo on the front page of *The New York Times*, a heartbreaking shot of refugees from Zimbabwe being shipped back home, out of South Africa. One of the refugees had a Yankees stocking cap on his head, the interlocking N-Y staring out above the sad face on a long journey. That same week in 2003, there was a photo in the *Daily News* of the so-called "Preppie Bank Robber" in Manhattan, caught on a security camera. The guy was looking down, wearing a Yankees cap. He looked a bit like Mike Mussina, except Mussina was with the team at the time, and so he had a pretty good alibi.

There were so many people wearing Yankees caps—here in New York, around the country, internationally, and maybe on several of the 120 or so extra-solar planets discovered thus far by astronomers—it was nearly impossible to keep count. The caps were like grains of sand on Orchard Beach. Neil Schwartz, the director of marketing for SportScanINFO, a retail monitor, said the Yankees accounted for 27 percent of all Major League Baseball hat sales in 2004, while the Red Sox were a distant second with 12 percent (followed by the Cubs, Cards, Braves, and Phillies). In a slumping sales market, the Yankees' cap and hat sales were up 33.24 percent from the previous year. They had the top three selling caps across all sports. The Tampa Bay Lightning's championship cap was fourth, while the authentic Red Sox cap was fifth. In the seven-day period ending with Labor Day weekend, retail outlets sold 10,300 authentic Yankees caps and well over 30,000 Yankees caps of different varieties. Even the hideous pink Yankees cap sold 4,200 units. Over the past six years, the Yankees sold more than 750,000 of their "basic 3-D" caps. That's just one model, and the numbers didn't count giveaways or knockoffs. A conservative estimate was there were more than 20 million Yankees caps, old and new, blue and pink, hanging in closets, folded inside drawers or sitting atop the heads of hairy and bald fans alike.

Some of these consumers were huge supporters. Others probably didn't even know a Yankee from a Dallas Cowboy. But the logo said something fashionable. It meant the city of New York, and to those in the know it meant winning in October. It meant you felt bigger and more empowered, somehow, when you put on the cap.

"People just relate that symbol with greatness," said catcher John Flaherty, who signed with the Yankees as a free agent from Tampa Bay. "When I first came here, Rick Cerrone, the public relations director, handed me the cap and said, 'Congratulations. This represents the most recognized symbol in sports.'"

The Yankees and George Steinbrenner were great at marketing this notion, at selling pride and excellence as if it were a Super Pretzel. They did it with Yankee-ographies on the YES network and with Monument Park and with the red, white, and blue bunting on the façade during the playoffs. They did it with the cap. By the end of October 2000, when the Yanks were beating the Mets for their fourth championship in five years, the Yankees had a piece of eight of the Top 10 selling licensed sports products in America. They were merchandizing kings. They were still kings in 2004, even after three seasons without a world title.

"The cap represents New York as a whole," Derek Jeter said. "People wear it who want something hot, who want something fashionable. We happened to have been hot the last few years."

There was pressure that came with the cap, with the logo, with the millions of people sold on a romantic notion of elegant supremacy. The Yankees needed to win some important games, starting in October, or the campaign and the caps would start to feel a little old. The image would begin to erode. It was hard to be the greatest franchise in the history of the universe if you didn't win a championship for four straight years, and then it would get a little harder to sell those caps, too.

You could feel that pressure on River Avenue, where the Red Sox and Yankees fans glared at each other as they passed. The

Tone516 and Domi lead the charge against this Boston fan by singing the Bleacher Creatures version of "Y-M-C-A" during the fifth inning. (Larry Palumbo/Coyote Magic Photography)

weather was changing, and it was more than Hurricane Ivan. It smelled like the postseason, three weeks early, even if this was just a relatively meaningless dress rehearsal. The Red Sox had been bragging, pride was at stake. The heavy hand and temper of George Steinbrenner was being felt everywhere. In the bowels of Yankee Stadium, clubhouse attendant and former Bleacher Creature Luis Castillo said he just wanted this series to end so things could get back to normal.

"Too much pressure," Luis said.

Luis (or as he preferred now, "Luigi") generally worked 13-hour days and was happy to do it. But today he was having a hard time finishing all the necessary chores. Players were bugging him for tickets. Their friends, relatives, and distant acquaintances had been bitten by the Yankees–Red Sox bug. The clubhouse needed to be inordinately neat because of possible inspections from higher-ups, and there was a huge media contingent standing around in the way, more than three hours before the start of the game. "Luigi" loved his job, and he planned to be back in 2005. But this part of it, the tense preparation, he could live without.

Funny how much difference eight days can make. On September 9, the Yankees had made up one of the Hurricane Frances games as part of an unscheduled day-night doubleheader against Tampa Bay. It was an 11th-hour juggling act, and when the game began in mid-afternoon, the stands looked emptier than Shea Stadium. Only a few hundred fans were on hand to watch Mike Mussina pitch superbly, finally, in a 9-1 victory, quite different than the average crowd of 48,531 the Yankees had been averaging. There was so little pedestrian traffic that Bald Vinny closed up his T-shirt stand early that day. Then he went into Section 39 where he was joined by only Little Mike, Old Man Jimmy, and one other Bleacher Creature regular, nicknamed Face.

"It was great," Vinny said. "The whole place was so quiet, you could hear the balls and strikes being called. You could carry on a conversation with the box seaters."

Obviously, that was not the case during this sold-out game against the Red Sox. Fans lined up impatiently along River Avenue before the gates were raised, and spectators filed in 98 minutes before the first pitch. Some of the Section 39 regulars were missing at the start of the game, scared off by forecasts of heavy rain from Ivan and by Sheriff Tom's dire meteorological warnings on the bleachers' website. Tina said her stomach didn't feel well enough to endure all these Red Sox invaders in the bleachers. She stayed home. Milton, as promised, was at the John Madden PlayStation competition, so there would be no cowbell in the stands. This act of defiance by Milton was greeted with uncommon rancor in the ranks. Yes, the Creatures understood that there was a $50,000 prize for the winner of the Madden competition, but it was generally believed that Milton had no better chance at winning that $50,000 than he would winning the jackpot of a million-dollar lottery. A message thread on the website demanded Milton's immediate resignation, and he eventually felt obliged to respond with his own post.

"I waited all year for this, and it's a shot to win $50,000!!! Unless you can give me a chance to win $50,000 for ringing the bell Friday night, you can [expletive]."

Milton also insisted there was a good chance he would be there in time for the start of the game, although he wasn't. He was clearly becoming sensitive to this type of criticism on the web.

"It would have been too hard to call me first, right?" Milton wrote, to those who had posted their critiques.

So Milton and the cowbell were missing again. Eventually the place filled up with all those blue and red jerseys. There was something almost refreshingly naïve about the Red Sox fans, who felt they owned the divine right to purchase a ticket, to sit in a Boston jersey next to the vaunted Bleacher Creatures of Section 39, and to get treated with genteel civility. That just wasn't going to happen. One woman in a Red Sox cap actually lamented that she couldn't purchase alcohol in the bleachers.

"You ought to be grateful, because you'd be dead if we could drink beer out here," Bad Mouth Larry informed her, performing what he considered a public service.

The usual professional wrestler impersonators showed up—Nature Boy, the Ric Flair imitator, sat in Section 37 and Stone Cold Steve Austin in Section 39.

"You want to see the Yankees open a can of whup-ass on the Red Sox?" the fake Stone Cold screamed. "Give me a 'Hell, yeah!'"

Soon enough, the regulars dredged up some old, reliable, nasty cheers sure to shock and offend the uninitiated.

"Schilling, your wife is ugly!" shouted Israeli Joe.

"Hit him in the head!" was the collective chant, when Manny Ramirez stepped to the plate and then again when Ramirez smacked a fake home run in the first (the ball curled, just foul) and took a fake trot around the bases. Johnny Damon was ordered by the Creatures to cut his hair, and then Statman decided that Kevin Millar "is a complete moron."

"Nobody in Boston listens to country music," he said. "What's with that 'Cowboy Up' nonsense?"

Statman had one wish, as he protected his precious scorecard from the impending rain: Just once, he wanted the Yankees to break out to an early lead against Boston, so that he wouldn't have to sweat out another tight contest. The thick lenses on Statman's glasses were fogged a bit from the 100 percent humidity and from the expected battle. He pointed out that during the 2003 regular season alone, the Red Sox had scored eight or more runs in seven of their nine victories against the Yankees. Statman was always pointing out things like this. That's why he was Statman.

"These games are too nerve-wracking," Statman said. "I'm tired of the high degrees of *agita*. You don't want to be pitching to Manny Ramirez with a one-run lead."

Once again, Statman's nerves would be frazzled. The Red Sox scored first, and then the rain started and the whole affair got dragged out miserably. Shirts, pants, and socks were soaked during a one-hour rain delay. When the skies cleared for a few hours, Olerud lined a solo homer into Section 37, and the Yankees went into the ninth inning with a 2-1 lead. Mariano Rivera entered the game, and in most cases you just knew that would be that. But Yankees–Red Sox games blaze their own trails, with uncommon twists and turns. Sure enough, Rivera blew the save when a broken-bat single dropped in front of a surprisingly non-aggressive Kenny Lofton in center field. Lofton was given the start in center by Torre over Bernie Williams, a move that was second-guessed in the bleachers and on many talk shows the next morning. Torre had made another odd managerial decision by starting Giambi, who clearly wasn't recovered from treatment on his benign pituitary tumor and who looked completely lost at the plate. Arguably, those judgments cost the Yankees the game.

When the ball bounced in front of Lofton, you could imme-diately see the difference in respect that Williams and Lofton com-manded on the Yankees. If that fly had dropped in front of Bernie, not a word would have been uttered—anywhere. But when it fell in front of Lofton, the fans were jeering and unforgiving, and Rivera himself turned to the outfielder, in an uncharacteristic tantrum, and mouthed, "Catch that ball!" Those words were painfully clear on television replays. Expert lip reading was not required.

The Red Sox won the first game of the three-game series, and the AL East lead was trimmed to 2½ games. The Yankees took the loss hard, although it clearly was no disaster. Winds and waters from Ivan blasted the area overnight, and then a new day dawned, clear as a bell. The plot turned more recognizable. The Red Sox had drawn blood early, but the Yankees would win the next two games. It was as if the rain, and as if Boston 3, Yankees 2, never happened.

THE BLEACHERS FAVORITE

For years, for what seemed forever, the fans gathered around the press entrance of Yankee Stadium hours before the start of home games to catch a glimpse of the players as they walked inside and to chat them up if the players were gracious enough to approach the steel barriers for some autographs. This was how Tina once got to know Bernie Williams and a handful of other players. But earlier this season there had been an incident in which a rambunctious fan clambered over one of the gates to get closer to a player. Ever since then, the barriers had been moved farther and farther away from the press entrance and from the players' parking lot. And now, since the Boston series, nobody could get closer than the Yankees boutique behind home plate, some 50 yards away. Nobody except the sportswriters. A handful of these unfortunate reporters were assigned, tonight and many nights, to hang out and wait outside for Steinbrenner to arrive and hours later for him to depart, so they could ask him to comment on the controversy du jour.

As Alex Rodriguez arrived in a black SUV for this game against Toronto, one sole fan, a woman, screamed in recognition from in front of the Yankees store, "A-Rod!"

That was it, the only interaction between player and fan in the Bronx other than some pregame banter around the dugout and the byplay between the outfielders and the Bleacher Creatures. It was a terrible shame, really. Other less famous and security-conscious teams encouraged their players to go out and meet with the spectators. The Yankees were about a decade and a billion dollars beyond that stage. They were determined to protect their expensive investments, even at the cost of intimacy.

The players still appreciated the New York fans, despite the limited contact. Gary Sheffield would be forced to miss this game after receiving a couple of cortisone injections for his sore shoulder and back, but he talked at his locker about how much the Bleacher Creatures had meant to him this season.

"They acknowledge everything I do, make it feel like big game after big game," he said. "This is the one thing you've got to experience, the way these fans are part of the whole scene. I recognize most of them by now individually."

Sheffield was having a wonderful season, good enough to earn "M-V-P" chants regularly from Section 39. In many ways, the timing on Sheffield's arrival in New York had been perfect. He hadn't taken Paul O'Neill's place but instead replaced that two-year interim parade of impostors. The fans in the bleachers were desperate for a strong regular performer out there, and they showed their support in a number of ways. Their chants, "Sheff! Sheff!..." had led several fans to wear a chef's hat almost every night. Sheffield was clearly committed to pleasing them, from the moment he tapped his chest with his fist on Opening Day. Sheffield didn't even want to miss this game against Toronto. He would have postponed those two cortisone shots if the Yankees hadn't won the last two games of their series against Boston. Half of him wanted to put them off, anyway. He dreaded the needles, he said. Despite the very public connection between Sheffield and BALCO, he insisted he hated drugs of any kind and that he lived in fear of doing damage to his liver and kidneys. Sheffield got the shots anyway and almost immediately felt no pain in the left shoulder that had troubled him so much. For the entire season, Sheffield was catching balls off to his side, rather than raising his left arm above his head.

"As soon as I got the shot, I didn't need a pain pill anymore," he said.

Sheffield would be back in the lineup the next night, hitting a home run, exactly the sort of performance that had endeared him to the Bleacher Creatures. He wasn't quite the crowd darling, though. Williams remained the Creatures' favorite, for his gentle temperament and his dogged longevity.

"It all starts with Bernie, as far as I'm concerned," Bald Vinny said.

If it hadn't been for Williams, there might never have been a roll call at all. Bernie was into it, despite his natural shyness, and nobody could forget Bernie's bobble head doll day two years earlier, when he performed a bobble head impression during roll call.

Not all the Yanks were so enthusiastic. When the Creatures tried to involve Joe Torre in the roll call, he politely turned them down by sending Luis Sojo up the dugout steps to wave in his stead. But most of the Yanks had come to appreciate the interplay, and they certainly understood the economics of the situation: The greater the attendance, the higher their salaries. The Yankees had just set another season attendance record this week during the Boston series, which meant that noise levels and salaries around the stadium would likely remain outrageously high into the foreseeable future.

"We get spoiled here," Torre said. "We get these huge crowds all the time. I like to think we're very comfortable here, and that our opponents are not."

The crowd was generally big, and it was different. Although fans at other parks reacted to circumstance, Yankees fans liked to think they were better than that. They anticipated and spurred the action. They created an edgy sense of momentum on their own, setting the stage for rallies and for strikeouts.

There would be no giant crowd and no sense of occasion at this anticlimactic game against the Blue Jays. All those hurricanes had played havoc with the late-season schedule, and this Monday night contest was a last-minute adlib. The Yankees were supposed to face Toronto on Tuesday, Wednesday, and Thursday. Now, the series would go Monday through Wednesday so that Tampa Bay could come back to the Bronx for a makeup on Thursday, which would start at the odd time of 3:05 p.m., with all tickets selling at a steep discount and revenues going to hurricane relief.

The pathetic attendance of 10,732 on Monday demonstrated that not even New York baseball fans were always capable of showing up on a moment's notice. Bald Vinny was doing lousy business at his T-shirt stand. His mind was wandering off to a recent landmark in his life, a decision to move into a new place in Queens together with Rose.

"I just hope we don't kill each other," Vinny said.

He had plenty of time to think about it, because nobody was there to buy his paraphernalia. The Yanks had pounded the Red Sox twice over the weekend, by a combined score of 25-5, after that disappointing loss on Friday night. Now they led by 4½ games, and with just 12 games left, it was getting tough to pretend that there was any race left at all. On top of that, Toronto was terrible, mired in last place after a disappointing season. So this hardly felt like an event in the Bronx, which was why Sheffield had decided to take his injections and miss a game, throwing the right field position open for a day.

Torre opted to put Kenny Lofton there, which was a slight act of disobedience because George Steinbrenner was in the house and suggested rather directly back in August that Lofton should never play out there in Babe Ruth's old stomping ground. Lofton had misplayed a liner and allowed a homer that probably wasn't catchable, by any reasonable standards—actions that caused Steinbrenner's proclamation. But Torre owned enough big victories in his reservoir to cool George's tantrum and the tantrum after that one. Torre started Lofton in right four more times since Steinbrenner's comments. As long as the Red Sox remained harmless in the rearview mirror, the lineup card was in the steady, empowered hands of the Yankees manager.

On a numbingly dull evening of baseball, the Yankees lost 6-3, and the Red Sox lost, and the viewers lost more than anyone. But it was important to get Lofton back into a game, as quickly as possible, wherever possible. He did well, too, making a backhanded shoestring catch on a sinking liner and doubling off a runner at first—even if both those outs were highly debatable calls by the umps. In a strange way, Lofton was still auditioning for a meaningful role on the Yankees, despite a solid enough .279 average and more walks than strikeouts. Lofton remained an outsider. That status was confirmed on Friday night in the ninth against Boston, when that bloop single dropped in front of him and when he'd been reprimanded by Mariano Rivera.

Torre said he hadn't heard of the controversy until later and that there was no way he was going to watch the replay to find out whether Lofton should have made a more direct play on the ball.

"It's not going to do me any good," Torre said.

But Rivera had focused blame on Lofton, who hardly seemed to notice. Torre benched Lofton for a couple of games and then picked him to start in right instead of Ruben Sierra, who was the designated hitter. Lofton had now played right field five times this season, and like most players could remember every one of those occasions. Baseball players own amazing memories, particularly for perceived slights. Thirteen years ago Bernie Williams had been stuck out in right field and he still remembered the horror.

Torre wasn't going to ask Bernie to do that tonight, just as he didn't ask Derek Jeter to move from shortstop to third to accommodate A-Rod. There were some veterans who were simply immune from such requests. It was tough enough on Torre when he moved Hideki Matsui from center to left. But Matsui was relatively new to the Yankees, and he understood in his own dignified way that he needed to pay some dues. In many ways, Lofton was more reminiscent of Rickey Henderson, oblivious, outspoken, and a little bit off key. His eccentricities were not mean-spirited, but they were barely tolerated on a team that prided itself on professionalism. At the advanced baseball age of 37 years, Lofton was somehow the mischievous youngest brother in the Yankees family. And on this night, Steinbrenner told the reporters standing outside the press gate he could tolerate Lofton in right and that he could put up with Torre's rebellious lineup card.

"That's fine, I don't care," The Boss said, before the game. "Because that is what Joe wants."

It was still an odd spot for Lofton, in the field and in the lineup. Lofton had 545 career stolen bases, yet he was batting last behind a lineup of turtles. As for right field, it was a direction where Lofton rarely bothered to gaze when he was in center. Willie Mays used to argue that center field was tougher because of the extra territory that needed to be covered. But the angles in right were difficult, and a fielder was playing in what amounted to a crowded corner directly underneath three decks of observers.

"It's totally different," Lofton said, about right. "You can't even explain it, because it's like there is a wall there that you don't look past and then the wall is gone and you're looking at something brand new. I played center field for 13 years. But God never puts you in a position you can't handle."

Lofton said he could handle it, same as the Babe, Roger Maris, Reggie Jackson, and Sheff.

"Babe Ruth had to see the ball, catch the ball, throw the ball no different than I do," Lofton said.

Things did not start off well for him. When Carlos Delgado lined a single out there in the first inning, the ball bounced off Lofton's leg and then he missed the cut-off man with his relay. No biggie. Delgado was still on first. Lofton calmed down quickly enough.

"It's like I say, 'The more you play there, the more comfortable you get,'" Lofton said.

Up in Section 39, there was another sparse showing by the regulars, who were already counting the days until they would all come out in force for the playoffs. Tina was there, sitting in Ali's old seat. She survived the final Red Sox invasion of the regular season and polished the plaque on her seat in memory of Ali Ramirez. Tina wanted Sheffield in right field, where he belonged. She didn't like Lofton, because he posed a threat to Bernie, everybody's favorite. She put up with the inconvenience, for one quiet night.

	1 2 3	4 5 6	7 8 9	R	H	E
TWINS	0 1 1	0 0 1	1 0 0	4	8	0
YANKEES	0 0 0	2 0 1	1 0 2	6	12	0

CLINCHING THE DEAL

T he regular season at home ended on a Thursday with great celebration and with the sort of game that could not have been more lyrical if it had been composed by Stephen Sondheim for Broadway. Milton was in the house at last—perfect timing. He banged on his cowbell, leading the chants and rallies. The Creatures were in fine form. Bad Mouth Larry had been thrown out the night before (by Terence Williams, of all people) for certain taboo gestures toward the box seats, but Larry was very careful not to get ejected this time, because it might be clinching night. And then the Yankees came back against Minnesota to win on a walk-off homer with one out in the ninth by none other than beloved Bernie Williams. It could only have been more perfect if Bernie's homer had landed on Tina's lap, instead of flying into the left-center field netting above the retired numbers.

The two-run shot clinched the AL East, laying the Red Sox to rest for at least another couple of weeks. And it was the Yanks' 241st homer of the season, smashing the franchise's all-time team record set in the fabled Roger Maris/Mickey Mantle heyday of 1961. The bleachers fans had grown accustomed to such dramatic flourishes, but they enjoyed themselves nonetheless. Meanwhile, the Yankees bathed in a champagne celebration inside their clubhouse. Joe Torre smiled and flinched, smiled and flinched, as his players took turns shaking and squirting the bottles over his head. Clinching a seventh straight division title, a 10th straight postseason, was tremendous fun. But it was also a messy ritual that "Luigi," the clubhouse attendant, quietly had hoped might take place this season on the road.

"Luigi" was now experiencing the mixed feelings that come with an unusual combination of menial work and great rewards. As the season wound down, the "clubbies" understood that the playoffs were around the corner and that their own financial situations would soon be affected by the success or failure of the Yankees. The champagne celebrations required a lot of preparation and clean up for these workers. There was the matter of sealing off each locker with plastic sheets (which featured corporate advertising, so that television cameras in the clubhouse would broadcast a free commercial on news broadcasts) and then cleaning up the place afterward. But each champagne party also represented a significant increase in bonus money. In 1998, after the Yanks' second

Bad Mouth Larry shows how he got his nickname by directing a barrage of insults at the right-fielder. (Mike Donahue)

Section 39 celebrates Bernie Williams's walk-off home run that clinched the AL East crown. In the background the Yankees celebrate at home plate. (Larry Palumbo/Coyote Magic Photography)

World Series championship in three seasons, there had been a gigantic windfall for "Luigi" and the others. David Cone, a generous man, was the team's player representative at the time and had successfully convinced the Yanks to vote one full share of the postseason bonus to the attendants, who would then split the prize. This translated into a $36,000 check for each worker. "Luigi" framed a copy of the check and hung it on the wall in his apartment before cashing the real thing. But when Cone moved on and Mike Stanton became the team's player representative, nothing was quite the same. The Yankees voted the attendants just one-quarter of a share, and in 2001 that had amounted to very little after the team was eliminated in the first round by the Angels.

The clubhouse guys were more hopeful this time, dreaming again of giant checks. In 2003, when Mike Mussina became the club rep, their share was increased to three-quarters, and the attendants figured they'd get at least that percentage this season, maybe even a full share. "Luigi" had his lobbyists, including Orlando Hernandez. He had done enough running around for these players, filling their pregame McDonald's orders, setting out their laundry, and even running out to cash their big checks.

"Some players leave right after the game, and they think that's what we do, too," Castillo said. "But then there are others, like Matsui, who stick around and understand how hard and how late we work."

All around the league, the clubhouse crews received a basic salary from teams but depended to a large extent on tips from these multimillionaire athletes. Not surprisingly, considering their income bracket, the Yankees were considered the best tippers in the league. The Red Sox were second. On the road, the more generous players would give $200 or simply hand over their per diem envelopes to visiting clubhouse attendants at the end of a trip. The major league per diem was $95, so that added up quickly. In return, these attendants performed all sorts of services for the players, above and beyond the call of duty. There were legendary adventures, too. One clubbie at Yankee Stadium supposedly took a visiting player's automobile to the car wash, after being told by the player that there was cash in the glove compartment to pay for the cleaning. When the clubbie opened the compartment, he was astonished to find that the stashed cash amounted to $80,000. That's what he told people, anyway, and it made some sense considering life among the economically enhanced.

This was now the world populated by "Luigi," the kid from the South Bronx. Just two days earlier, it appeared that the Yankees would never clinch the division at home, that he would be spared, and that they would go down to the wire with games at Toronto. The Red Sox and the weather weren't cooperating for Torre, and neither were the Yankee pitching arms. The Yankees had escaped Fenway Park after winning one game and losing the next two to Boston, badly. They were three games ahead with six to play.

The Yanks were set to begin their three games against the Twins on Tuesday, when the remnants of yet another hurricane, Jeanne, worked their way up the East Coast and turned the Bronx into the Everglades. Four inches of rain poured down, most of it beginning in late afternoon, and it was evident that this game was not going to get played. Night games generally were scheduled to start in the Bronx at 7 p.m., far more convenient than the 8 p.m. starts of the 1980s. The games had simply grown too long for such late beginnings, because of between-inning commercial interruptions and endless pitching changes. It didn't matter what time this game started, though, it wasn't going to happen. Everything was flooded. A doubleheader was set for the next day, for Wednesday. These postponements and rescheduled games were disheartening for fans, and now clearly the Yanks were not going to max out their attendance record. Steinbrenner would have to settle for a franchise season mark—3,775,292, the league's highest (the Yanks also led the league on the road, attracting 3,308,666). In the clubhouse, though, "Luigi" knew that he was going to get home early and that this rainout was an unexpected treat.

"Bad for the fans, good for me," he'd said, laughing.

On that soggy evening, one of his chief backers and benefactors, "El Duque," was scheduled to start against Minnesota. Hernandez was such an effective starter since the All-Star break, his reputation had been enhanced and so was his political power in the clubhouse. That had to be good for "Luigi," the bilingual whiz kid. "Luigi" and "El Duque" were both hustlers in the nicest, most earnest sense of the word.

But then on Tuesday, Hernandez's name wasn't in the lineup posted on the wall. Instead, Jon Lieber was scheduled to start this game that never got started. The clubhouse media, desperate for a rainout story, had a big one—yet another crisis in the rotation. With a week to go until the playoffs, there had been only these two reliable, hale, and hardy starters in the fragile Yankees rotation, Hernandez and Mussina. Then Hernandez came into the clubhouse with a big bag of ice on his right shoulder, and there was only one. His shoulder was tired, nothing more, "El Duque" kept saying. He'd confessed this to the team trainer, Gene Monahan, on Monday. He was scratched from the mound on Tuesday. Soon enough, there was a deep halo of reporters around his locker. Hernandez bristled at what he said were the same questions, over and over.

"I can't say the future," he said.

But this was an important shoulder, exact age unknown, and the regular season was growing short. The writers wanted details, prognoses, schedules. Hernandez wouldn't and couldn't. He said he didn't know, and he was surely telling the truth. How can you predict what the tendons and muscles will do tomorrow, or the day after, or for Game 4 of the AL Division Series?

Torre and Mel Stottlemyre were forced to make more decisions, always more decisions, none of them pleasant. They would monitor "El Duque" carefully. Torre would juggle and nurture these fading arms with no time to spare. The manager had to figure out whether Hernandez was fit, whether Kevin Brown and his broken hand were an option (that didn't look good), and whether there was a way to use three starters instead of four when none of those three was particularly durable. The truth of the matter was that the average age of the starting rotation was now about the same age as the ridiculously young general manager, Brian Cashman, who was 37. Brown was 39, Mussina was 35, Lieber was 34, and "El Duque" was anybody's guess. Only Javier Vazquez was a relatively youthful 28, and his status was growing more tenuous by the mediocre outing.

Despite the deluge of rain and question marks, Torre took everything the only way he knew how, in stride. These were the arms that were dealt him. They weren't the sturdiest of missile launchers. The Yankees let too many of those escape before the season started, and then they didn't sign Curt Schilling, who would have wrapped up the division about a month ago. Schilling or Roger Clemens, one or the other in pinstripes, and there would be no hand-wringing in New York at the end of September. But anybody who felt sorry for Torre, for this ever-expanding payroll (nearly $150 million more than Minnesota), wasn't looking around the league very carefully. The Yankees weren't the only ones with pitching problems. The slumping A's couldn't figure out what happened to their ace, Mark Mulder, who was 0-3 with a 7.71 ERA in the last month. The Red Sox were dealing with a star, Pedro Martinez, who had recently melted down and referred to the Yankees as his daddy. The Twins, who always had enormous trouble with the Yankees, were shortening their rotation to three starters in the playoffs. They couldn't find a fourth. Minnesota really wanted one pitcher, Johan Santana, to pitch every inning, but the playoffs weren't constructed that way.

You didn't get to start Mussina, Clemens, and Andy Pettitte every October. Sometimes, you had to adlib a little, and it was good for the soul. The Yankees still owned the best one-two bullpen punch in the world, in Tom Gordon and Mariano Rivera, an astounding offense, and every reason to believe they could survive this latest crisis, Hernandez' shoulder.

"We don't think it's that dramatic," Torre insisted. "He doesn't think it's anything major."

Hernandez had been an unexpected midseason gift horse from out of the past. He'd dazzled for a couple of months and given the Yankees reason to believe in him again, but there were never any extended warranties that came with the shoulder. Now the Yankees were like most teams that were heading into the playoffs, which meant they didn't really know where their next start was coming from. They needed seven innings from somebody, or from some tandem, before they handed the ball to Gordon and Rivera. Too many people had become convinced that Hernandez was invincible again, that Señor Octubre was going to give them one or two of those vintage outings every series. Not necessarily.

"It's worrisome when the pitchers have trouble and the play-offs start next week," Torre said.

When the season began back in April, the Yankees already had joined the real baseball world, the one without the jaw-dropping rotation or the killer ace. They compounded their shortcomings, trading for Esteban Loaiza. Now they had a week to scramble, to find some innings, to oil the shoulder of "El Duque" and to tinker with Brown's brain. The Yankees were searching for answers in all the wrong shoulders.

Outside the stadium on Tuesday the rain was pouring and the place was deserted. River Avenue was so empty it might as well have been Roosevelt Avenue outside Shea. Stan's wasn't doing any business, and Vinny's T-shirt stand never opened. It was one last quiet moment before things got crazy again. Two nights later, the place was alive and nutty. The Yankees clinched the division on Thursday. By Friday morning, there was a huge line outside the stadium for playoff tickets. The Creatures didn't have to worry about that. Their tickets arrived in the mail, as part of the convenient season package. They would all start showing up again in Section 39, every one of them, because these games counted now, and it sure looked like the Yankees could win or lose any of them. The debate began about their chances immediately.

"No one has the pen we do," The Dever believed. "Our starters may not line up like Boston or even the A's, but if we keep the games close and get to their pens, we always have a chance. Other teams can't say the same about us. So let Schilling throw lights out. Once he gets yanked, we will do damage to Foulke or any of the middle relievers they have. Last year, we didn't hit. We need our bats to get our starters a lead early, then take the lead into the eighth so our pen can hold it and win the game for us."

The nature of the Creatures, however, was to fret, and so another fan dug up the bullpen stats for the five contending American League teams and found out the Yankees pen had the highest ERA among them. Didn't matter, Bad Mouth Larry insisted.

"We have a few lousy relievers skewing those numbers," Larry said. "Our bullpen is one of the best."

It would take three more days for the Yankees to finish the season on the road at 101-61 and to find out they would be facing Minnesota in the division series. Boston was set to play Anaheim. Johan Santana (20-6), a legitimate Cy Young candidate, would start against Mussina in the opener. Santana owned an uncommon range of velocity on his pitches, baffling hitters with fastballs in the mid-90s and change-ups in the low-70s. He had pitched twice against the Yankees this season, with significant success. He'd allowed just three runs in 12 innings for an ERA of 2.25, struck out 11, and held the Bombers to a batting average of .182. Santana could only throw so many innings, though. The Yankees had whipped the Twins last October in the first round. They'd owned the Twins again this season. A bit of the old confidence and bravado returned to Section 39. The Creatures were ready. Yes, the rotation was a mess, and Torre couldn't name his Game 3 or Game 4 starter. But even if the Yanks were beatable, the fans figured, they weren't going to get beaten by Minnesota.

	1 2 3	4 5 6	7 8 9	R	H	E
TWINS	0 0 1	0 0 1	0 0 0	2	7	0
YANKEES	0 0 0	0 0 0	0 0 0	0	9	0

ALDS
GAME 1

I t didn't make a lick of sense. The Yankees had sold out about 20 games during the regular season, and their crowds had averaged more than 40,000. Now the playoffs came, the same throngs were showing up, and suddenly security was quadrupled in and around the stadium. Police were everywhere—on horses and on the sidewalks and patrolling the stands. Credentials were triple-checked. Rules that were never enforced during the previous six months were suddenly carried out to the letter of the law. Vendors were harassed; tailgaters were tailed. Was Osama Bin Laden only interested in disrupting the playoffs, not the regular season?

It was like this every postseason, an umbrella of strict code enforcement extending from the Major Deegan to River Avenue. Up on the roof of the parking deck by the elevated subway tracks, Blue Lou was told by a park ranger to stop grilling chicken and ribs at his pregame barbecue or else she would issue him a citation. There was some kind of citywide rule against charcoal grilling in non-designated areas, yet another good argument against building a new football stadium and luring more tailgating fans into the five boroughs.

"This is why it's tough to be a Yankees fan," Blue Lou moaned. "It costs $20 to park, you can't drink legally, you can't even cook."

For nearly a decade now, for 10 straight playoff runs, the Bleacher Creatures had been chased around the South Bronx neighborhood and out of their favorite haunts for pregame festivities. Back in 1995 they would gather at the running track across from the stadium to drink some beers, sitting by the long jump pit also known as the Sandbox Suites. Or else they would walk to a rocky area in the back of the park to quietly smoke some weed. Then police started using the park as a staging area, closing it to the public before and during games. The Creatures moved to what they dubbed Crackhead Park up the hill or hung out in the basement of an area bodega. That didn't last long, either. A slew of tickets chased fans from their various havens. They tried to gather in parking lots and on sidewalks. There was a hide-and-seek game going on with cops and rangers on the tops of parking lot roofs. The Creatures had their alleyways and hiding spots, but there was no denying the police owned a distinct judicial homefield advantage. The Bronx courthouse was just up the hill to the east of Yankee Stadium, and the county jail was just a couple blocks to the south. A guy could be cuffed, tried, and incarcerated all within half a mile of Yankee Stadium. This was a fairly intimidating layout, if you stopped to think about it.

Cheering for the Yankees was supposed to be like rooting for U.S. Steel or Microsoft, you kept hearing. But it was harder than that, especially in October. It was tough because of all the police harassment, and it was tougher because of the pressure. The Yanks had won 26 championships in the 84 seasons since 1920, when they got Babe Ruth from the Red Sox. That sounded like a lot, but it amounted to less than one championship every three seasons. Statistically speaking, the Yanks won only 31 percent of the time. The other 58 seasons, or 69 percent of the time, the years had finished badly for them, just as they did for fans of other franchises. Most recently, the Yanks had failed three successive times to win the title, in disheartening fashion—a ninth-inning collapse in Game 7 against Arizona in 2001, a quick dismissal by Anaheim in 2002, and a startling loss to Florida in 2003. Yankees fans expected no sympathy from outsiders, of course, but they also didn't want to hear about how they were spoiled rotten by all the success. There were bad endings lurking out there, same as for anybody. Up on the parking deck, the fans felt like they were targets.

"Why can't the rest of the league just divvy up the other portion of championship seasons and be happy with it?" G.B. Steve Krauss wondered.

"As Yankees fans, we are allowed to be arrogant, because we pay a price. If one thing goes wrong, every Mets fan I know calls me up," Midget Mike said, contemplating the burden that is a baseball monopoly.

"Twenty-five times they're wrong, and then the one time they're right they come out of the woodwork laughing in your face," Mike Donahue said.

Frankly, all the high expectations were not entirely fair for the Yankees players, either. Baseball wasn't basketball. The best team didn't always win the big game. A pitcher on the lesser team could get hot, and a ball could drop in front of an outfielder. You played best of five in the first series, which wasn't enough. If you split Games 1 and 2 at home, a measly two-game losing streak on the road finished you off in a hurry. Then there was this three-tiered playoff system, filled with ambushes at every turn. It had been a minor miracle when the Yankees managed four titles in five seasons under this format, a feat unlikely to be replicated for some time.

But those were the rules, and the Yankees had managed just fine with them from 1996 to 2000. They fared so well, people in New York forgot that Steinbrenner once went 17 seasons without winning a championship, the longest drought of any single Yankees owner in the franchise's history. Everybody knew what was expected of the pinstripes. The pressure came with the cap, with the logo, with the millions of people who were sold on a romantic notion of elegant supremacy.

"We shoot for the best, not just for being a good team," Derek Jeter said.

The best of the best. That's what the ads said. And now it was time for the Yankees to put their bats and gloves where their caps were. Up on the parking deck, the Creatures gathered at the barbecue to trade stories and postseason predictions. The fretting never ended. The latest annoyance was Johan Santana, a pitcher who changed speeds on his pitches as easily as most people changed socks. G.B. Steve figured the Yanks were playing with house money in Game 1. If they beat Santana, the series was over. If they lost, the American League Division Series would just go exactly like the previous season against the Twins, with three straight Yankees victories after a freakish defeat.

But you never knew, so everybody reported to the bleachers with their A-Game, even Milton, the cowbell man. Milton took some well-deserved heat for skipping the two key Red Sox games, one to bang his bell on national TV during the NFL draft and the other to chase the $50,000 grand prize in the video game contest. Needless to say, Milton didn't win the $50,000.

"I won three games, but I needed five more," he said.

He was clearly unrepentant, as he took his dented cowbell out of its sack. It was in horrible shape.

"Imagine how bad it would look if you came to more than four games a season," Bad Mouth Larry scolded him.

Milton mounted an effective defense. He brought up his three kids and his wife again, and soon enough everybody forgave him his trespasses. It felt like family night out there. Bald Ray was talking about his new grandchild, his fourth one at the tender age of 47. He offered a kiss up to God for such blessings. Midget Mike was professing his love for Suzy, a bleacher gal who was also a preps sportswriter up in Westchester County.

Suzy had been a Section 39 regular for about five years, an extraordinarily long shelf life for any woman. She chalked it up to being "one of the guys" and knowing her baseball. When she first showed up there, Suzy happened to mention that she was Albanian. Then she revealed her last name was Lulgjuraj, the same as Tina Lewis's maiden name. It turned out they were related, distant cousins, and a bleachers bond was formed. Suzy required the sisterly support sometimes, because she dated a couple of the Creatures. There were harsh breakups and feuds along the way.

Tina showed up on this first night of the playoffs, limping badly. Her back was out now, after she'd slipped on the floor of the apartment where she was staying. It was always something. Blue Lou had not entirely forgotten his feud with the press, it turned out. On the trunk of his car, he hung a plastic squid, an ink-squirting symbol of his anti-media splinter group. But everybody seemed in good spirits, ready for a fresh October. The Creatures had paid dearly for this quest. Bleachers tickets to the first round were a reasonable $12, but a $6 handling charge was attached to each of them. Altogether, a single postseason strip of tickets cost $550. Bald Vinny bought one for himself and one for his girlfriend, Rose. That amounted to $1,100, on top of his 2004 regular-season ticket of $648 (he also planned on buying Rose her own regular-season package for 2005), which was why he would be selling T-shirts for many years to come outside Stan's on River Avenue. The hunt for championship banner No. 27 was costing a lot of people a lot of money, not only George Steinbrenner.

Inside the stadium, separate from the bustle and surveillance outside, the place took on its special October aura. The red-white-and-blue postseason bunting was always a wonderful touch, like wreaths at Christmas time. The emerald field gleamed more in the postseason, because the night around the building was darker this time of year. The networks wanted all the Yankees playoff games on late as showcase events, during primetime, unless the popular Chicago Cubs were also in the playoffs. The Yanks' classic white uniforms reflected the light from the overhead lamps, showing off those pinstripes.

On this occasion, Torre trotted out his most dependable lineup for Game 1: Leading off and playing shortstop, the team captain and proven leader, Derek Jeter; batting second and playing third base, Alex Rodriguez, who was now supposed to start earning that giant contract of his; batting third and playing right field, Gary Sheffield, who had just told a *Sports Illustrated* reporter that he'd used a steroid ointment two years earlier prescribed by Barry Bonds's personal trainer; batting fourth and playing center, Bernie Williams, the last link to the 1995 bunch that began this 10-season playoff run; batting fifth and catching, Jorge Posada, too often overlooked and underrated; batting sixth and playing left field, the quiet, understated, and arguably most consistent Yankee, Hideki Matsui; batting seventh at designated hitter, the reinvented Ruben Sierra, who had become such a favorite dugout presence lately that he was chosen by Torre to manage the final regular-season game; batting eighth and playing first base, John Olerud, the late-season acquisition who had provided a steady glove where the ailing Jason Giambi once stumbled around artlessly; batting ninth and playing second base, Miguel Cairo, an office temp who turned into the nicest surprise of the whole year; pitching (why did there have to be pitchers?), Mike Mussina, the best of a sad lot of slumping or aching Yankees starters.

The lineup looked fine, but it didn't work. Nothing worked against Santana, who got a lot of help from five double plays and Torii Hunter in centerfield. Hunter made one perfect relay home and later climbed the wall to steal a possible homer. As rallies fizzled early, the mood in the stands turned ugly. It was exactly as that great bleacher poet and prophet, Paul Kaplan, always predicted: When there was no common enemy for the Creatures, they would turn on themselves. The problem was there were just no "T-C" caps in sight, no Twin fans to be found. They were refusing or were unable to report to New York for their ritual hazing. There weren't that many transplanted Minnesotans living in New York, and tickets were tough to come by anyway. Without a worthy target for their taunts, the Creatures did what they always did without an obvious dartboard. They turned on themselves like cannibals.

The Dever, Bald Ray, and Blue Lou were furious with Nature Boy, who had a long history of bugging Section 39 with his insane rants. He was bringing too much attention to himself again in the heat of competition.

"I hate that guy," Mike Donahue said.

Blue Lou decided that Nature Boy was not taking October seriously enough, that his Ric Flair "Whoo!" schtick was okay for the regular season but not for the playoffs. So Lou confronted Nature Boy about this, got in Nature Boy's face, and Lou was evicted by security guards in the third inning. Blue Lou had toiled for three hours cooking at the barbecue and had been the perfect host, and now he hadn't made it through an hour of the first playoff game. A lot of the Section 39 regulars blamed the incident on those upstarts in Section 37.

Nature Boy does his Ric Flair act for the fans in the stands. (Larry Palumbo/Coyote Magic Photography)

"Section 37 is a joke," Tone Capone said, analyzing the brush-fire afterward. "They didn't watch a single pitch until about the fifth inning, they were so busy listening to Nature Boy. They're the quintessential Yankees frontrunners, that whole section."

While 39 warred with 37, FourDogg4Life made the case for Section 41 (thankfully, there were only four sections in the right-field bleachers, or this could have gone on forever).

"Listen to Nature Boy in 37 or you can sit in 39 while the drama of an ALDS game in the eighth inning unfolds right before your eyes, and your season could come to an end, and you hear the same tired old songs," FourDogg complained. "For this fan, I am content sitting in Section 41 where we actually watch the game and enjoy each other's company. We are not media whores like the 39 bunch—not all of them, but you know which ones they are. There is still another reason to sit in the bleachers... to watch a baseball game."

So there were those feuds going on, and the Yanks were losing to the Twins, and then Midget Mike was arguing with Dan Mofsenson about an $18 ticket that Dan sold Mike for $25.

"Not my fault you don't have a ticket," Dan said. "I've been burned so many times before, I'm just trying to get back some money."

"Friends don't do that to friends," Mike insisted.

Somebody suggested that maybe Mike was nobody's friend, but that was beside the point. Dan argued he wasn't scalping the ticket, that he could make much more than a $7 profit if he put the ticket up for sale. Money was tossed to the ground. Feelings were hurt. And then the Yankees lost the game on top of everything.

Across the continent in Anaheim, the Red Sox were crushing the Angels 9-3. This was not the way October was supposed to start. Blue Lou had wasted an impressive illegal barbecue.

	1 2 3	4 5 6	7 8 9	10 11 12	R	H	E
TWINS	1 2 0	0 0 0	0 2 0	0 0 1	6	12	0
YANKEES	1 0 2	0 1 0	1 0 0	0 0 2	7	9	0

ALDS
GAME 2

There was really no reason to panic after the opening playoff loss, if you heeded history's recent lessons. The Yankees had now dropped the first game of the ALDS in four of the last five years, and the only time they'd won the opener in that span was the only series they'd lost, to the Angels. So you'd think there would be some perspective about the Game 1 loss to Minnesota. But the pre-Game 2 tone around River Avenue was pretty grim.

You wanted a bad omen? Somebody threw himself under a train on the IND subway line, according to both police and MTA Joe (who always knew the inside story at the Metropolitan Transit Authority), causing serious commuting delays to the stadium.

"Jeez, we're only down one game," said Mike Donahue, the cynic, wondering what would drive a person to such a desperate act.

Things were getting ugly, and there below the elevated train in all his smirking glory was undercover cop Tom, the archenemy of all Bleacher Creatures.

"A sweep!" Tom predicted, and he was talking about the series, not about a drug bust. "No Andy Pettitte to rescue them. By Sunday, we'll be locking up Bald Vinny."

The cop was kidding about Vinny, of course, but there was enough fretting to go around. Bald Vinny brought his entire inventory of T-shirts to the game, just in case this was the last home game. He also began announcing plans for a Halloween costume party. By now, reports of this book were surfacing, causing another stir. Bad Mouth Larry had posted a couple of possible cover shots on the bleachers website, and not everybody was happy. Midget Mike was particularly incensed that Vinny was one possible cover.

"I'm his friend, but the Creatures are not about this," he said, pointing to Vinny's stand in front of Stan's. "They're not about marketing. They're about craziness."

It was the game that was truly crazy this time, another one of those desperate last stands by the Yankees. They fell behind 6-5 on Torii Hunter's homer in the top of the 12th. If they lost, realistically, the Yanks were cooked. But they came back to win on an RBI double by A-Rod and a sacrifice fly by Matsui that scored an aggressive Jeter from third. There was no shortage of heroes. A-Rod went four for six with a homer and three RBIs. Jeter led off the game with a homer and then scored that instinctive game-winning run by tagging up on Matsui's short sacrifice liner and dashing to the plate.

As Bernie Williams would say, "This team in the postseason—there's something about this team that never ceases to amaze me."

There was a great sigh of relief in Section 39, a sense that this had been the definitive turning point in the series. The inexperienced, inexpensive Twins had lost their moment and their momentum. They had eased against the wrong foe, the same way that archvillains always underestimated the escape prowess of Batman. When Jeter crossed the plate, there was great celebration in the right-field stands, a temporary truce between all feuding factions. Very temporary. Because as it happened, a reporter for the *Minneapolis Star-Tribune*, Paul Levy, had interviewed several of the Creatures that night for his paper. And in his article published the next day, Levy unwittingly created a giant controversy among the bleachers fans by calling Vinny the "head Bleacher Creature."

Vinny had not declared himself the head Bleacher Creature, but it was a natural leap of logic for the reporter since Vinny led the first-inning roll call and was arguably the most visible fan. Immediately, there was an extensive and sometimes heated website debate on the subject of group leader. Bad Mouth Larry argued that Tina was still the queen of the bleachers, and it was a shame that some of the newcomers didn't recognize that. Sheriff Tom Brown also took some offense at a few of the comments. He

G.B. Steve celebrates the Yankees scoring in Game 2. (Larry Palumbo/Coyote Magic Photography)

launched an eloquent and bittersweet diatribe on the tide of change and the nature of rooting in the bleachers.

"I am not looking for pats on the back, or a plaque, or anything," Sheriff Tom wrote, "but to sit here and be disrespected after my tenure out there is appalling to me, and I thank people like Larry for throwing a little cold water of reality to the face of it all. For 10 years I don't think there was one other person with the patience and tolerance out there that would simply welcome anyone, open his doors to anyone, or school them on 'the bleachers way.' And now I come on the board to read that it is all over for me. I sat there 'til the final out with the Yankees up by 10, or down by 10, knowing I had 90 minutes door to door 'til I could get home to do the whole thing again the next day, and the day after that. Everyone started going to the bleachers because of the Yankees. Most of us stayed there because of the people we sit with. We can watch the game anywhere, in or out of that stadium. No one is out there for simply the view. If it wasn't for the people I would bleed for out there, circumstances would have seen me leave the bleachers years ago. I wish [my daughter] Emma took more of a shining to the Yankees, and baseball in general. But she gets bored with baseball on and goes back to playing with her toy farm and Wiggles dolls.

"A reporter is not going to cite someone as the head of the Bleacher Creatures unless that person is somehow painting himself that way," Sheriff Tom continued. "Over the years, Milton has been painted with that brush, Tina, even me. It could be simply how you carry yourself during the interview or the pride you show in what you are talking about. Let me put it this way: If I was still out there 60 times a year, any talk of who runs the bleachers would run through me. I have been asked dozens of times if I ran the place. The difference with me and some others out there is I always said no. I would much rather have been the straw that stirs the drink for the place as it used to be, than be the guy running the show now. So if you think the winds of change you are mentioning hurt me, keep in mind the winds that blow now carry a stench."

And there it was—Tom's long, pinstriped journey told in retrospect—from proud boozing fan to prouder family man. Vinny would defend himself and try to undo the damage of the Minneapolis article. Vinny was the first one to admit he enjoyed media coverage, if only because it was great for business. But he really felt badly about the way he'd been portrayed, as spokesman and leader.

"I am sure that my business as well as the roll call stuff just puts me more in a public eye," Vinny explained. "People see me there every day and know that is what I do. I have missed only three games all year, and I am constantly stumping for the bleachers to every newbie and tourist that comes into the section [and I am the only one to fully admit that I am a media whore]. Half the people out there do their best to offend and try to scare off the new people. I try to be helpful and friendly to new folks [for the most part]. Without new people, all the tired old jokes and gimmicks that everyone hates [but still make everyone laugh each night] would just disappear.

"Just for the record, if it wasn't for Tom, I would never have been part of this group. There is no head guy, there are no initiations, there are no dues," Vinny continued. "You don't get a membership card or a newsletter. There is no formal organization or criteria for membership. There are just several hundred, if not thousands, of people who enjoy the atmosphere that was created by a core group of passionate [and mostly funny] people. If I was in the shoes of Tom, Tone, Steve, Tina, Kaplan, and a whole host of others, I would be pretty proud to say I helped contribute and shape something that makes so many people happy."

On it went, this political jockeying and diplomacy. The Twins would be dispatched in Minneapolis, with two straight Yankees victories. The Red Sox were heading toward the Bronx. The bleachers were about to overheat from all the excitement. It was a good thing the Red Sox would be coming in next, because clearly the Twins were not enough of a diversion to rescue the Creatures from a self-centered implosion. The Creatures thirsted for a real challenge. They also needed to rediscover their inner naughtiness. Marc Chalpin complained that behavior was becoming much too civilized out there in Section 39, like business in a corporate boardroom, and that only Tone 516 and Midget Mike were keeping things interesting.

"Show me something rowdy," Marc said, desperately. "Jesus Christ, it's like a church choir out there. Don't tell me you can't get away with stuff. Just don't call a security guard a whore. That's a bad move."

Always a bad move, but now more than ever. You didn't want to get thrown out for the next series.

	1 2 3	4 5 6	7 8 9	R	H	E
RED SOX	0 0 0	0 0 0	5 2 0	7	10	0
YANKEES	2 0 4	0 0 2	0 2 X	10	14	0

ALCS
GAME 1

O utside the stadium before Game 1, the streets were turning into a real freak show, as they always do for Yankees–Red Sox. There was a guy in a giant sombrero carrying a banner for the Bronx Bombers, there was a pinstriped car cruising River Avenue, there was a man waving about 50 flags, and there was Uncle Sam, or at least someone dressed like Uncle Sam, with a wad of play money in his pocket. There weren't that many Red Sox fans, though. They must have had trouble finding tickets, because otherwise you figured they would have killed to be here. Curt Schilling was pitching Game 1, and in one of his more boisterous moments had promised to shut up 56,000 New Yorkers at Yankee Stadium.

"Nothing makes me happier," he'd said.

It was exactly that sort of confidence (plus Boston's impressive three-game sweep over Anaheim) that had caused most experts to pick against the Yanks. After 39 American League pennants and 26 championships and after dominating and enforcing The Curse on the woeful Boston Red Sox for 86 years, the Yankees somehow found themselves the betting underdog in the AL Championship Series. The very idea that the Red Sox were listed as favorites going into Game 1 was proof enough for Connecticut Joe that Vegas was losing its tenuous hold on pseudo-reality.

"It shows drugs have made their way out there," said Connecticut Joe.

Joe predicted that Bubba Crosby would become this year's Aaron Boone, because his name started with "B" and he was just obscure enough to drive Red Sox fans insane. Most of the Creatures found it something of a relief not to be favorites, for a change. The Yankees as underdogs! Now there was a concept.

"This is like Tom and Jerry, all over again," said Mike March, a.k.a. Knoblauch. "We always know Jerry wins, same as the Yankees."

Still, the bookies figured this would be Boston's best chance at toppling the pecking order and maybe its last opportunity for some time to come. Who knew what would happen to the Red Sox after this season? Pedro Martinez was scheduled to become a free agent, while Curt Schilling would turn 38 in November. The confluence of age and talent on that Boston roster meant time was ticking, loudly. A Yankees victory would be historically decisive and all the more delicious.

The buildup for this series was predictably over the top. It was impossible for New York papers not to seize on Pedro Martinez's "daddy" comments, and so the back page of the *Daily News* by cartoonist Ed Murawinski featured Babe Ruth calling to his kids, "Come to Daddy." The Red Sox players were drawn as the kids, in diapers, and were lucky not to be pictured bawling their heads off. Murawinski had once done that to Newt Gingrich, and Gingrich never recovered politically.

All the Creatures came for this one. Midget Mike complained, of course, that he was sick of the Red Sox.

"This series is so played out," he said. "It's boring listening to Red Sox fans. I can't stand listening to them."

Donald Simpson came, too. He tried to stay overnight in Harlem whenever there was a Yankees home game, because the commute from his new home in Brewster was just too long, especially during rush hour. He'd missed a few more games than in past seasons, but overall he was enjoying the leafy suburban life in upstate New York. His back was no better, no worse. He'd won yet another legal case and was awaiting more money. No matter what his health or circumstances, the only millionaire in Section 39 was not going to miss the Red Sox. Nobody was going to miss the Red Sox. Donald had a new girlfriend, who worked at the United Nations (the same place as Bald Ray) and watched these games with him in the bleachers. They were becoming a celebrity bleachers couple, same as Rose and Vinny. Donald was no fool. He knew the Red Sox, with Schilling and Martinez, were a real threat this postseason. He also figured that their hopes would be smashed, in the fine tradition of this rivalry.

"The Curse overcomes everything," Donald said. "This is their best shot to win, and they should win, but they won't. That's what will make this so sweet."

The issue before this game, as usual, was where the Creatures would congregate to talk baseball, get inebriated, and mock Red Sox fans. A barbecue had been tentatively scheduled for the rooftop of the parking lot, but the fear was that police would initiate a crackdown against tailgating and all forms of parties. Cops were outside the old bodega, a block east of the stadium, handing out tickets to customers as they walked out with open beer bottles or cans. When it came to Yankees–Red Sox games, all forms of pregame enjoyment were frowned upon by law enforcement. Police didn't want incidents, and Yankees–Red Sox usually meant problems. The bleachers fans had learned the hard way in 2003 that drinking their beer out of cups, instead of bottles, was not enough to avoid citations during the ALCS.

"Last year we were busted, and the beers were in cups," Sheriff Tom said. "Come to think of it, the time before when I got busted, you guessed it... the beer was in a cup. The cops don't want alcohol. And when Boston is in town, they smell trouble, and they will root it out. Just my two cents. You think I would want to spend $30 to $40 for six beers in two hours in a bar before the game? Hell no. Will I? To avoid these cops, hell yeah."

Tom suggested the Yankee Tavern or the News Room, near the old bodega hiding spot on Gerard Avenue. Stan's was just too crowded. But Midget Mike and Mike Donahue couldn't resist the proximity of Stan's. They went inside for beers, arguing about whether Columbus Day should be a holiday.

"It just proves the Creatures will argue about anything," Bald Vinny said.

Vinny was uncharacteristically nervous, though not about the series itself. A Red Sox–Yankees meeting meant a windfall to his business. Vinny's new T-shirts, picturing Babe Ruth with the words, "Pedro's Daddy," were selling like hotcakes. But there was a downside that came with such a hubbub. A year ago, during the Red Sox–Yankees playoff series, Vinny had been busted by cops for not having a vendor's license. The laws were very complicated, and Vinny had most of them covered. He had his vendor's tax ID. By paying rent to Stan's, he was selling under the aegis of that emporium. Legally, Stan's could sell its wares on the sidewalk, as long as the merchandise was within three feet of the storefront. But in 2003, Vinny was nailed with "obstructing pedestrian traffic," because he lacked the license. It cost him a lot of hassles and $100. So Vinny was busy this night being very nice to every patrolman in the area, including undercover cop Tom, the archenemy of all Bleacher Creatures.

Tom was predicting a seven-game victory by the Red Sox, with Pedro Martinez the winner in Game 7.

"It's going to happen right here," Tom said. "Then we'll see the Creatures crying, going back to New Jersey where they come from."

Vinny was forced to smile, graciously, while Tom spoke about a Red Sox victory and how Queens, where Vinny was from, wasn't really part of New York.

Once Game 1 began, everything was different, a long celebration and an endless serenade of, "Who's your daddy?" A Red Sox cap was confiscated from some poor Boston soul and then cut into tiny pieces for souvenirs. The Yanks jumped off to an early 2-0 lead in the first inning, and it became obvious that Mike Mussina had all his stuff going. Mussina was perfect through six innings, mowing down 18 straight batters from one of the most fearsome lineups in the league. By then, the Yanks were up 8-0, and a good night's sleep appeared assured. But that's not how these two teams play against each other, and before long the Red Sox had closed the gap to 8-7 in the eighth. "Enter Sandman" blasted over the public address system, and Mariano Rivera came jogging to the mound.

This was no ordinary Superman appearance for Rivera. He'd been through emotional hell over the past three days. After the

Yankees wrapped up the ALDS and just before the champagne celebration in Minneapolis, Rivera's wife, Clara, came into the visitors' clubhouse to tell Rivera in front of a few teammates that her
cousin, Victor Dario Avila, and her cousin's 14-year-old son,
Leonel, had been electrocuted in a pool at Rivera's estate in
Panama. Rivera flew down to Puerto Caimito, where he attended
an emotional two-hour funeral service at the church, Dios de la
Profesia. Rivera promised Leonel's mother he would take care of
her and of everything, and then Rivera headed on a plane back to
New York for Game 1. He reached the stadium by police escort in
the third inning and was in the left-field bullpen by the fifth,
receiving hugs from teammates and supportive chants of "Ma-ri-
a-no..." from the Creatures.

Nobody knew what to expect from Rivera after such a terrible
ordeal. He was remarkable. He came in with two outs and the
tying run on third in the eighth, and he forced Kevin Millar to
pop out and end the inning. The Yanks pushed two more runs
across in the bottom of the eighth, and Rivera again stopped the
Red Sox in the ninth. The game ended about the way most of
Section 39 figured it would go, which is the same way the last 86
years had been going. There were a few potholes near the end, but
then Rivera filled them. Only the nonbelievers in the crowd were
ever sweating. Midget Mike decided the series was basically over
now that Curt Schilling had lost.

Mike Donahue had been very busy all day, smuggling four
ounces of vodka into the stadium inside a hollowed-out cell
phone, arguing that Columbus Day should not be a holiday,
because Columbus basically missed his target of America ("It's not
like he sailed up the Hudson," he said). Donahue decided now
that he needed bigger fish to fry. He wanted Red Sox nuts Matt
Damon and Ben Affleck to know they had an open invitation to
visit and film Section 39, and that they would find the Bleacher
Creatures extremely videogenic.

	1 2 3	4 5 6	7 8 9	R	H	E
RED SOX	0 0 0	0 0 0	0 1 0	1	5	0
YANKEES	1 0 0	0 0 2	0 0 X	3	7	0

ALCS
GAME 2

J oe Torre was a remarkable manager, a calm rudder in any storm at sea and an engrossing storyteller. But there wasn't much mischief to the man, and he had an aversion to the chaos and edginess of a large audience. He was of an older generation that expected crowds at baseball games to behave themselves—maybe not like at Sunday service, but like at the church picnic afterward. Torre would surely be offended if he sat among the libertarian chanters in Section 39. He would be horrified to know that when the Creatures went on a road trip to Toronto in 2002, the game was stopped momentarily because they were reflecting light into the eyes of Blue Jay batters, using free lunch boxes that were handed out by the host team as promotional gifts. Torre's dignified presence demanded some basic decorum. So while many Yankees players such as Gary Sheffield and David Cone truly enjoyed the interplay between themselves and the wilder fans, Torre preferred to hang out with a few good friends and keep his distance.

Torre understood that the giant raucous crowds at Yankee Stadium were a financial necessity and that they created a very real home edge for his team. Torre wasn't about to take them on, not in the fashion that Lee Elia once did in Chicago, leading to that manager's dismissal. But Torre also wasn't going to walk up to the top step of the dugout to wave at the Creatures or play their games. You got the feeling, frankly, he didn't want to be associated with the riff-raff. Before Game 2, in the press room dining area where interviews took place, Torre was asked about how Yankees fans might intimidate Pedro Martinez with their inevitable "Who's Your Daddy?" chants. Torre basically issued an apology on behalf of the Yankees, in advance.

"I just think it's part of the deal," Torre said. "I had a concern yesterday that we feel safe where we are. You know, I have a sense that we're safer in the dugouts than the people that are in the stands because of the passion of it all and with the chants. Sometimes it gets a little foul, which, you know, I don't think anybody is crazy about, and people find that funny. The only thing that concerns me is that, yeah, it's a baseball game, it's passionate, and it's warlike sometimes, but it's such a great rivalry that you certainly don't want it to become ugly. The fans are a big part of making it a wonderful time, but I think it's still our responsibility to let them know that it's 'Let the games go on,' and not contribute or take away from them."

While Torre was fretting inside the stadium, a grand costume party and freak show was gathering out on River Avenue. A truck for the local strip club, Sin City, was parked near the bleachers' entrance. The sides of the truck were painted with near-naked women in provocative poses, hardly a sight that Torre or George Steinbrenner would endorse during Yankees playoff games. The fans walked past, hardly noticing. This was no time for such carnal distractions. They'd come to bury Pedro Martinez, not to praise him.

Everywhere you looked, there were banners and posters referring to Pedro's "daddy" comments. Martinez was a funny and ironic guy, but if he could have taken back that one quote, he surely would have done so. Instead, he had thrown raw meat to the lions. Everybody wanted a piece of Pedro. There were grown men, Yankees fans, dressed in diapers with the words, "Same crap since 1918," written on their bottoms. There was another guy with a rattle and a fuzzy baby hat, getting his photo taken by every New York newspaper.

Bald Vinny had his share of interviews lined up, too. *USA Today* was doing a piece on him, and a photographer from that national newspaper was lurking about, working the angles. Vinny's lawyer had made him available to Channels 2, 4, 5, 7, and 12. Meanwhile, Mike Donahue came by with quite the confession: The Section 39 stalwart would be committing a demographic crime today, sitting in the box seats behind the Yankees' dugout. An old frat brother had offered the ticket to him, and Donahue had accepted. Just like that, he would cheer alongside the enemy, the rich guys. He didn't even sound remorseful.

"The weather is changing, and my voice is cracking, so I can't be heard all the way from the bleachers," Donahue insisted, pathetically.

Nobody believed this, least of all Donahue. Mostly, he just wanted to get Gary Sheffield's batting glove, if Sheffield tossed it over the dugout. Donahue was a glove sniffer of the worst kind. It was questionable whether Donahue would survive the whole game on his elegant throne, considering how he stuck out like a sore middle finger. In the box seats, he could buy beer from vendors if he wanted. But just from habit, he was smuggling in three beer cans, wrapped up like a fake deli sandwich. He also had his trusty vodka in a fake cell phone, and some weed tucked into a secret pocket of his pants. You could take the Creature out of the bleachers, but you can't take the bleachers out of the Creature. Sure enough, Donahue got into trouble in the box seats. One of the young men in his group said it was his birthday. The fellow proved it by passing around his driver's license, and it was at this particular moment, coincidentally, that Donahue discovered the birthday guy was a Red Sox fan. So Donahue did what he had to do. He threw the driver's license onto the field. By the fourth inning, Donahue was ejected. In another example of twisted stadium justice, the guy whose driver's license was thrown on the field was also ejected. This led Donahue to consider himself a hero. One less Red Sox fan in the ballpark.

"I fell on the grenade and took one for the whole platoon," Donahue insisted.

There were others like Donahue, former Creatures, also sitting all over the park, betraying the bleachers in this class warfare. Pops had left the bleachers long before, heading for the upper deck because of the beer ban. Cartelli was last seen behind home plate somewhere, sneering at his erstwhile brothers across the park. It was their loss, most of the Creatures figured, just as this game would prove to be another Boston defeat, the second straight. Jon Lieber, the very hittable Yankees starter, pitched brilliantly for

Milton continues to champion a Yankee 2-0 lead in the ALCS on River Avenue. This would be the last celebration for the fans until 2005. (Larry Palumbo/Coyote Magic Photography)

seven-plus innings, allowing only three singles and a walk. All that worry by fans about Lieber was for nothing. He was superb. Pedro wasn't bad, really. He pointed up to the heavens when the fans asked him, "Who's your daddy?" He kept his composure most of the time, although he walked four and gave up a two-run homer to John Olerud. That was more than enough to sabotage the Red Sox again.

Mariano Rivera came in from the bullpen with two outs in the eighth inning. He'd had his troubles with the Red Sox during the regular season, blowing two saves, but he still looked untouchable against Boston in the postseason. The Yanks won 3-1, and there was now a sense that the great Red Sox threat was ebbing and that all the hype of the season had created a false sense of doom. Not only had the Yanks defended their home turf in Games 1 and 2, but they had beaten both Boston aces, Schilling and Martinez. Even more telling: Schilling's future status was in doubt. Before the game, it was announced that a dislocated tendon in his ankle was popping out and couldn't be stabilized. Schilling was questionable for Game 5 and, come to think of it, so were the Red Sox.

	1 2 3	4 5 6	7 8 9	R	H	E
RED SOX	0 0 0	4 0 0	0 1 0	4	11	0
YANKEES	0 0 0	0 0 0	1 1 0	2	6	0

ALCS
GAME 6

By the time the ALCS had reached Game 6, nerves were torn and friendships were frayed. It was now conceded among the Creatures that the Red Sox were a real threat to ruin everything and to embarrass the Yankees and all their fans with a historic comeback. No team in baseball ever had returned from three games back. No team even had managed to tie a playoff series from three back. This scraggly Boston bunch (who might have been kindred spirits to the bleachers fans if not for the uniforms) was making life miserable for everyone in Section 39.

The last two marathon games in Boston ended disastrously, uncharacteristically, as the Creatures watched their beloved Yankees go down in clutch situations, time and again. In Game 4, the Yanks led by a run going into the ninth, three outs away from sweeping the series. Torre called in Mr. Reliable, Mariano Rivera, to nail down the save. Rivera walked Kevin Millar. Pinch runner Dave Roberts stole second, and then Bill Mueller drove in Roberts with a liner right up the middle. Rivera wound up face down on the mound, talking to the dirt, while the tying run crossed the plate.

In Game 5, the Yanks might have won in the ninth inning if a deep drive by Tony Clark hadn't climbed over the left-field fence on the bounce, becoming a ground-rule double instead of an RBI double. On it went like this. Alex Rodriguez homered in Game 4 but failed to come through in Game 5 when he might have won the series with a single swing. His strikeout in the eighth with one out and a runner on third was brutal. Derek Jeter, who knocked a base-clearing three-run triple in Game 5, had laid down a sacrifice bunt in order to set up that failed RBI situation for Rodriguez. Several writers took note about what Jeter had done for the team and then how A-Rod had let him down. There were also some menacing rumblings in Boston that Curt Schilling was being fitted for a new shoe, plus new stitches inside his ankle, that would enable him to start Game 6 at close to top form.

While the Yanks were busy blowing Games 4 and 5 at Fenway, the bleachers fans gathered at a couple of Manhattan saloons, watching the two meltdowns on television and dying slowly inside (not just from the alcohol). Some of the fans went to Jeremy's Alehouse, the recently renovated bar at South Street Seaport. The moment that worn-out Yankees reliever Paul Quantrill came into deadlocked Game 4 in the 12th inning, Bad Mouth Larry wisely advised everybody at Jeremy's to chug their beers and get ready to go home. The bar staff started locking up and lowering the gates, even before David Ortiz's homer won the game for the Red Sox. Sure enough, Quantrill did what Quantrill does worst.

By Game 5, factions clashed, and a splinter group headed to a different bar, Timeout, on Columbus Avenue. Some of the Creatures were fed up with Jeremy's, for a couple of reasons. A few (though not all) of the fans felt the hospitality at Jeremy's was not quite the same as in the past. Relations had suffered a bit since the fight back in 2001 involving the Creatures and a Mets fan, who was a friend of Jeremy's. A change in supervisory personnel didn't help. So there was some sense that the fans' special brand of enthusiasm was resented at Jeremy's now. But also there was another problem. It turned out that even bleachers fans had entourages and that they were not always welcomed by the other more established entourages.

"It's bad enough there are newcomers [to the bleachers]," Tone Capone complained. "Now, the newbies have newbie friends. They're just annoying."

These upstart visitors to Jeremy's annoyed the core Creatures with their parasitic behavior. Basically, they were eating the free buffet provided by Jeremy's staff without purchasing any liquor.

"Look, some people are always going to have cash issues," Bald Vinny said sympathetically.

The trouble was, these hangers-on were not tipping the staff, either, which was the cardinal sin of freeloading.

In any case, everybody was now in the bleachers for Game 6, putting up with each other's eccentricities and with the Red Sox and the weather. It was misty, drizzly, and cold in the South Bronx. People's socks were getting wet, always a miserable situation. Bald Vinny postponed the opening of his T-shirt stand so that his inventory would not get soaked. Then the game started, and things grew worse. All those bad rumors about Schilling were true. He was ready to pitch. Schilling, the man who had promised to silence all Yankees fans, was doing just that. Orthopedists had somehow constructed some Frankenstein shoe for the guy, and the doctors had patched up that ankle of his with stitches. Now he was shutting down the Yanks.

The Yankees' desperation showed on the field. In the eighth inning, Rodriguez knocked the ball out of Bronson Arroyo's mitt while running to first, trying to beat out a grounder. A-Rod was initially called safe, but then that was reversed after a lengthy conference of umpires. This was infuriating to the Creatures. They had been part of enough collisions in and around the benches in Section 39, while chasing batting practice homers, to figure that it was only right and natural to knock the baseball out of somebody's hand. The umps decided, however, that A-Rod had gone well beyond the natural motion of a base runner, while banging Arroyo (who had hit Rodriguez with a pitch earlier this season). Not only was Rodriguez called out, but Jeter was forced to return to first base, which was where he was when the play started. Instead of having runners at first and third with one out and down two runs, the Yanks had only Jeter at first and two out. Another rally was doomed.

The stadium fans took this badly, tossing garbage of various sorts onto the grass and down into the bleachers from the upper deck. It was hard to tell what happened on the field, exactly, from Section 39. But everybody was incensed. For one of the few times in his rooting career, Milton was a little bit scared of the situation in the stands. He had brought his son with him, and the mood was growing ugly. In the last few rows of the bleachers, fans who the Creatures had known for years were suddenly throwing everything

Riot cops stand between the bleachers fans and the field after a controversial play in which Alex Rodriguez slapped the ball out of Bronson Arroyo's glove. (Larry Palumbo/Coyote Magic Photography)

they could grab. One projectile, a two-liter soda bottle, struck the legs of a cop.

"The crowd was going nuts. I didn't want my son hit in the head," Milton said. "I had to try to calm everybody down."

Terry Francona pulled his Red Sox players from the field back into the dugout. A ring of menacing riot cops invaded the warning track areas. Some of the cops climbed into the bleachers for a half inning. Most of the garbage reaching the field was not coming from the bleachers, which were recessed behind a handicapped section and were carefully supervised. The core Creatures were sick and tired of the bad reputation that dogged them, and in the scrutiny of October they resisted their natural instincts to fight back. The fans were still trying to figure out exactly what happened on the play and why Jeter was sent all the way back to first base. A bleachers fan can't really see the scoreboard replays, because the angle is so bad. Milton just figured that A-Rod had done something desperate.

"In the heat of the moment, he was still the new Yankee trying to prove something," Milton said. "It got to him, like it did to Roger Clemens when he threw the bat at Mike Piazza. Your instincts since Little League are to swing at the glove. It wasn't a dirty play, though. Dirty is if you hit him in the face."

The mood of the fans did not improve when the Red Sox finished off the victory 4-2, tying the series at 3-3. Suddenly, there was little talk of Blue Lou's planned World Series barbecue on Saturday. Panic of a sort set in. On the Creatures' website, co-host Baloo ran a banner proclaiming that the Yankees sucked and that this series was over. Tone Capone, another moderator on the web page, felt compelled to step in and remove Baloo's post, a form of necessary partisan censorship. Capone returned a good-luck photo of Bernie Williams to the site.

The picture of Bernie gave the Creatures faint assurance, heading into a Game 7 on Wednesday. Everything the fans had fretted about during the long regular season, particularly the shoddy rotation, was coming home to roost. It was not comforting for any Creature to know that Torre would be handing the ball to erratic Kevin Brown, the guy with the stiff back, the broken bones in his hand, and the inscrutable personality, to beat the Red Sox in the biggest game of the season. But Brown was really all that Torre had, beyond a sore-armed "El Duque" and the unpredictable young Vazquez.

Baloo was right. Things looked bleak.

	1 2 3	4 5 6	7 8 9	R	H	E
RED SOX	2 4 0	2 0 0	0 1 1	10	13	0
YANKEES	0 0 1	0 0 0	2 0 0	3	5	1

ALCS
GAME 7

Until now, there hadn't really been that many Boston fans buzzing about Yankee Stadium for this series. But Red Sox supporters smelled history, and they came to Game 7 in bunches, like red locusts to a plague. If the Red Sox were going to slay The Curse of the Bambino, then these famously suffering Bostonians needed to witness firsthand such a sight. They paid absurd prices to scalpers or to anybody standing around with cardboard in his hands. They wanted inside, and they wanted revenge, not necessarily in that order. Thousands of them roamed River Avenue behind the bleachers' entrance on Mickey Mantle's birthday, trawling for tickets. They required their rapture after 85 years of miserable anticipation.

The Creatures were accommodating, to a degree. If they had extras, there was an irresistible profit to be made. Connecticut Joe sold four bleachers tickets (face value, $51 apiece) on eBay to Red Sox fans for $1,150. The purchasers told him they'd be heading down to the Bronx to pick them up, just before game time. Another Red Sox fan drove around River Avenue in a van, with signs on his windows that said, "This is our year."

"That car's going to have four flat tires after the game," Mike Donahue said. "It's going to be up on blocks."

There was a good deal of such gallows humor going around. Undercover cop Tom was walking past, patrolling the sidewalks, putting his hands around his own neck, joyously predicting the final act in an epic Yankees choke. Among the Creatures, there was some discussion about what would be worse: losing a big series to the Mets or to the Red Sox. The vote was split on this one. Bald Vinny thought losing to the Sox would be worse, if only because his inventory of anti-Red Sox T-shirts would take a hit. Donahue said that losing to the Red Sox might mean the world was coming to an end and that he believed Nostradamus had mentioned it somewhere in his prophecies.

"It would be like Charlie Brown kicking the football," Donahue said. "It would be like the Joker getting Batman."

Midget Mike, a contrarian to the bitter end, argued that it wouldn't be so terrible to lose to the Sox, that the Mets fans were always worse. In 1986, he said, he pulled for the Sox. In 2000, he lost sleep until the Mets were dead and buried. Mets fans were intolerable. Midget Mike already had received a couple of phone calls in the morning from Mets fans, alleged friends, telling him to "get ready" to lose.

"I don't really hate Red Sox fans that much," Midget Mike said. "I'm just sick of them. There's a difference. Mets fans are always in your face."

If the Yankees lost, Bald Vinny joked that he would have to flip over and burn some cars. Donahue said he'd head to Interstate 95 and start smashing windshields with a bat. Neither was serious, of course. But the thought of losing to Boston, especially after such an impossible collapse, was terribly distressing. The impending disaster had brought the Creatures together, drawn some of the old guard back, and sparked discussions about odd characters from the past. It soothed the nerves to speak of less anxious times. Miles, a former sportswriter with *The Village Voice* and a longtime Creature, suddenly appeared on River Avenue after a two-year absence.

"Force of gravity pulled me here," Miles said.

He was looking for a quick ticket but soon gave up the hunt. Miles was due back at a bartending job in Brooklyn. His brief visit inspired a trip down Memory Lane among the Creatures, who remembered fondly those Section 39 comrades who'd moved away or fallen by the wayside over the past decade. There was Sandy, who had warred with Tina, a battle that can never be won. There was Kaplan, who still made cameo appearances but was now far too skinny to be rolling around the benches during the seventh-inning stretch. There was George, who settled in Israel. There was Bald Teddy, who moved to Kansas to further his teaching career.

There was Chico, the bleachers' bookie, and Jodie Foster (a look-alike, actually), and Rob Andrade, the bleachers gigolo who was always juggling bleachers girlfriends. There was Cartelli, who had been a rising star in the bleachers and then suddenly abandoned the place for more expensive seats.

"He was our Kevin Maas," Donahue said. "Such unrealized potential…"

And there was Vanessa, considered a definite "hottie" by the bleachers crew.

"You don't get too many women like Vanessa," Donahue said, wistfully.

If only such sweet nostalgia could last forever. But eventually, it was time to file inside the bleachers and pray that Kevin Brown harbored one great Yankees moment inside him. The Creatures had good reason to mistrust Brown, the hired gun and the guy who already had shot himself in the foot a dozen times this season. It'd been a lousy year for Brown. He messed up his back, then he slammed his left hand into the wall, then he apologized, and then he just plain stunk. New York believed in the guy even less than his teammates did. This giant game against the Red Sox was going to be a final precious chance for Brown to rewrite the ending to his tale and to make all the pain and all the self-loathing go away for a night and an off season. With one solid start, he could muzzle the demons deep inside and then spend four months knitting his broken bones while watching redemptive tapes from Game 7.

Five innings, Joe Torre hoped and prayed. If Brown would give the manager five decent innings, then maybe Torre could keep the Yanks in the game with a patchwork quilt combination of starters and relievers. But Brown walked stiffly to the mound and immediately showed everyone why he was not Roger Clemens, proving again the Yankees had thrown their $15.7 million per season at the wrong guy. Brown lasted 1⅓ innings, gave up five runs, and cut the hearts right out of the Yankees. Give him this much credit: Brown was bad so quickly, he never allowed fans to pretend he would be good. He yielded a leadoff single to Johnny Damon in the first inning and couldn't even take advantage of a brilliant relay by

Derek Jeter to cut off the first run at the plate. Brown gave up another single to Manny Ramirez, and a homer to David Ortiz on a pitch he meant to keep low that crawled up into the fat part of the strike zone.

The next inning, Brown was worse. He loaded the bases, walking two guys, and then Torre and Mel Stottlemyre had seen enough. They brought in the next firestarter Javier Vazquez, who was costing the Yankees about $9 million this year for his middle relief work in the playoffs. Vazquez's very first pitch was lined by Damon into the right-field box seats for a grand slam—a decisive blow that could never be softened or reversed. The Red Sox owned a six-run lead and the worst fears about this Yankees team were realized. They didn't have the pitching, period, because Brown and Vazquez weren't Clemens and Pettitte.

That had been Brian Cashman's theory, remember? Brown would be Clemens, only not semi-retired and not living in Texas. Vazquez would be Pettitte, only younger. Whenever the Yankees execs sat down and wrote the obit for this season and began planning for 2005, Cashman would have to begin by figuring out what to do about Brown and his contract. Brown wasn't just a mystery. He was a dark cloud in the clubhouse, and he was to turn 40 before the next Opening Day. If there was one thing a team required from its starters, it was reliability of performance and character. With Brown, you never knew whether he was going to pitch or commit hara-kiri out on the mound.

The Creatures tried, they really did. Almost everyone was there (Tina was oddly absent). Game 6 had been a quiet, sullen affair. So the bleachers fans went out of their way to make noise early in Game 7 and to get the juices flowing. But once the Yanks were down by six runs, something strange happened out in the right-field stands. A sense of inevitability took hold in Section 39, along with an eerie serenity. The game and the series were now so out of reach, the bleachers fans were forced to adjust to a new reality. The Yanks trailed 8-1 after four innings and 9-3 going into the ninth, when a lot of Yankees fans left to avoid seeing Red Sox players hugging each other on Lou Gehrig's infield.

"The Yanks were out of it so early, people didn't even get really upset," Bad Mouth Larry said.

The Creatures that remained kept rooting as if nothing wrong had happened, as if this were a game against the Tigers in mid-May. There was no panic, no edge. Milton banged his cowbell. Over in Section 37, Nature Boy led his "Whoo!" cheers. There was nothing the fans could do about this disaster, and they were just happy that most of the Red Sox fans in the stadium were congregating around the third-base line.

The game went on like this, hopelessly, and then it was finally over, around midnight. Soon it was Thursday, October 21, no longer Mantle's birthday. Somebody joked that it must now be the birthday of Horace Clarke, the Yankees' longtime second baseman during the team's dark ages in the late 1960s and early 1970s. There had to be a logical explanation for the impossible.

The Red Sox had beaten the Yanks, four games to three. Pigs flew. Hell froze over. All that stuff. The *Daily News*' front-page headline would scream, "The Choke's on Us."

After the loss, in the clubhouse, "Luigi" was running about, cleaning and packing. He wouldn't get his big windfall, no World Series share. At his locker, Derek Jeter issued no excuses. He simply reiterated this Yankees team was no longer the same bunch that had won those four titles in five years. Jeter, Rodriguez, Sheffield, and Matsui had averaged .491 the first three games of this series. They'd averaged .167 in the final three games against a bunch of ragged, tired Boston pitchers. Then there was the Yankees pitching, which had yielded 41 runs in this series. A reporter half expected to find an outline of Kevin Brown's fist in the clubhouse wall. But that wasn't the Brown who was in there. This Brown was sad and reflective. He was just resigned to his own frailty and mediocrity.

"I'm not angry," Brown said, standing at his locker. "It's not like I've left any stones unturned. I did everything I could to be the pitcher I was last year. Short of trading the health of my family, I'd do anything to go back and give this team a chance to win.

Some of the Bleacher Creatures were freaking out when the Red Sox beat up on the Yankees in Game 7 of the ALCS. Big Joe's despair was the most emotional and unrestrained. (Larry Palumbo/Coyote Magic Photography)

I simply just was not there. I wish I'd been the guy I'd been in the past, at least one more time. I couldn't make pitches."

That was the scene inside the bowels of the stadium. Outside, the stands were cleared, except for hundreds of Boston fans who couldn't get enough of the celebration. And yes, except for a few of the Creatures. They hugged; they said their goodbyes. They promised to see each other soon and to talk each other off the ledge, when this despicable turn of events could be dissected from more emotional distance. Somehow, life would go on.

The 2004 season hadn't been a total loss. Far from it. New friends and relationships had been forged. Tina was still cancer-free, more than a year after her diagnosis and treatment. Donald had adapted to rural life and to home ownership. Milton, still searching for a good-luck cowbell like the one he had in 2000, was coaching his kids. Bald Vinny had sold more than his share of T-shirts and was ready to move in with Rose.

The Creatures headed back out onto River Avenue, back into their existences outside Section 39. If the Yanks had won, tradition demanded a party under the elevated tracks behind the bleachers' entrance. Not now. The fans talked about getting new starting pitchers, about maybe signing Carlos Beltran, about traveling down to Florida in March for spring training, and about reordering season tickets for Section 39. They would be back and so would the Yankees.

Nobody ever said that being a Bleacher Creature was a sure thing. It was just the closest thing to heaven, without a guaranteed championship every October.

EPILOGUE

In the days and weeks that followed the Red Sox debacle, the Yankees would remake their rotation with acquisitions such as Randy Johnson, Jaret Wright, and Carl Pavano while each Bleacher Creature required a personal grieving period to reconcile himself or herself to the new baseball landscape, the new post-October reality. After beating the Yanks, Boston went on to sweep the St. Louis Cardinals in a one-sided and rather lackluster World Series, to break the 86-year-old curse, and to celebrate with a raucous parade. Curt Schilling was everywhere on the television, sneering at Yankees fans, thanking God, and telling people to vote for George W. Bush in John Kerry's very own state. The next season's schedule was already published, and the Red Sox would be raising their championship banner in a game at Fenway against the Yankees. Facing these harsh facts was a very individual process, a painful necessity if bleachers fans were going to look forward again to the next season with fresh eyes and eager hearts. The inevitable winter transactions would surely help, but in the meantime there were deep wounds to be healed:

Donald Simpson retreated to his home in Brewster to rest his back and his nerves.

"Like a bear in hibernation," he said. He was still shaking his head about Game 4 in Boston. "I don't know… one game… three outs… Mariano on the mound. I was very upset. This is two years in a row we had a team celebrating on our field, and then to have it be Boston…"

Donald said very few people would see him over the next few months—maybe his girlfriend, Rekiya. Donald was smarting.

"It's all going to be a little tainted now," he said. "I hope The Boss will do something about the pitching. I'm hoping Boston will make a mistake [and] sign all these players just because they won."

Because he was quiet certain it would be a long winter, Donald had his fireplace inspected. If nothing else, he would be warm and toasty while dealing with his sorrow.

"I'm going to put on a fire, burn some demons," Donald said.

Bald Vinny was a resilient Creature and a true entrepreneur, and he was already busy with several new projects. Just two weeks after the Red Sox disaster, his mind was far from October 20. He was moving into his new place in Astoria, Queens, with Rose. The apartment was just 20 minutes from Yankee Stadium, closer than his old apartment in Forest Hills. Vinny was trying to sell his precious black leather sectional couch to somebody—anybody—on the Bleacher Creature website, but there were no takers. He would probably put it in storage. Vinny was also making preliminary plans for new lines of T-shirts. He was thinking of something like, "See you in 2090," which would be exactly 86 years again after the 2004 Boston championship.

"Thankfully, I sold out of the '1918' shirts," Vinny said. "I have a few 'Pedro's Daddy' shirts left. The thing about T-shirts is, they don't have an expiration date."

He had hoped to host a Halloween party for the Creatures, but then Vinny became immersed in all the chaos of moving. He gave up on the idea. He was sad about that—about the way his friends in Section 39 hurriedly said goodbye after Game 7. It happened so abruptly, without reason or enough warning.

"Nobody wanted to leave the bleachers," Vinny said.

Midget Mike Milianta was monitoring the Bleacher Creature website, www.section39.com, which now featured the logo, "Ichoke." Whenever some pie-eyed fan insisted that the Yankees were not chokers and that they should be proud of their season, Midget Mike set them straight. To one such poster, Midget Mike responded with a list of choking Yankees:

1. Gordon choked the entire ALCS!
2. Mariano choked in Game 4 being three outs away from a sweep!
3. A-Rod choked with one out and a man on third!
4. The entire lineup choked Games 5, 6, and 7!
5. Brown and Vazquez choked in Game 7!
6. I'm tired of typing this!

In other words, we choked, stupid!"

Luis Castillo, a.k.a. "Luigi," had taken the loss harder than any-body, probably harder than any Yankees player or coach. When he helped Derek Jeter clean out his locker, Jeter had told "Luigi" he still couldn't believe this was happening. "Luigi" could-n't clear his mind of that memory—that dreadful sight. For days afterward, he seriously contemplated quitting his job as clubhouse attendant. When the Yankees lost, Castillo knew he would have to put up with endless teasing from at least two sources: his good friend and former Yankees pitcher Ramiro Mendoza, now with the Red Sox; and from Pookie, the Red Sox visiting clubhouse manag-er. After Game 7, "Luigi" went into the Red Sox clubhouse to con-gratulate Mendoza.

"There he was, soaking wet with champagne," he said. "He hasn't stopped calling me since."

Even when the Red Sox were down two games, Pookie prom-ised "Luigi" that the series would be coming back to Yankee Stadium and that Pookie was saving a 1918 bottle of champagne for the celebration. All these things were rattling around the atten-dant's head.

"I can't sleep," he said, weeks after the series loss.

"Luigi" wouldn't know until December the size of bonus check from the Yankees' postseason, but he knew it would be a far cry from the $36,000 he got in 1998. He had been hanging with Ruben Sierra, his new best pal, trying to find some solace in the defeat. He decided he would stay on as clubhouse attendant.

"I'm not quitting," he said. "But I wish it didn't happen. It was hard to have happen. Can you imagine the game next April in Fenway Park? They'll be waving their banner in front of us. They act like they've won five championships in a row. It would be great to see Boston not even make it to the playoffs the following year, the same as Anaheim and Florida."

Milton Ousland was a cowbell man for all sports seasons, and he had seamlessly moved on to his other rooting interests, the Knicks and the Jets.

"Surprisingly, I recovered very quickly," he said. "The Yanks gave me four championships, they beat the Mets, and I find it hard to get upset for a long period of time after a loss, the way I used to. I can't get mad now, because George [Steinbrenner] gave us so much since the 1980s."

It was Milton's theory that the loss to the Red Sox was good for the league and the rivalry, which had been too lopsided before.

"This spices it up a little," he decided.

Milton was spending more time with the kids, and he also had his own way of wreaking revenge on Red Sox fans. Milton was addicted to online sports games, and he took particular glee in beating Boston opponents at baseball video games. Milton didn't like to beat them while playing as the Yankees, because that was too easy. He preferred to humiliate them while managing an inferior makeshift team. Milton hadn't decided yet whether to purchase a new cowbell for the 2005 season, although it was clear the 2004 bell had done the Yankees no particular good.

Tina Lewis had her reasons for missing Game 7 at Yankee Stadium, and they had nothing to do with her health, which was fine. She had a feeling, a bad premonition, her beloved Yankees were going to lose to the hated Red Sox, and she didn't want to be there to witness such a thing.

"I just knew from the beginning of the season," Tina said. "I know these things."

So instead of going to Section 39, Tina had paced the sidewalks around her apartment in the Morris Park area of the Bronx. She tried to avoid hearing the result, but she ran into a friend, Stan, who gave her a partial score. It wasn't good. She heard the final awful news from MTA Joe.

"Don't even tell me," she said.

But he did, and that was that.

"I took it really hard, but I'm a smart person when it comes to baseball, and I can tell you we lost because Joe Torre did not manage the way he is supposed to manage," Tina said. "Everybody was hitting for the fences. Everybody was aiming for a home run. There's no heart out there. No Paul O'Neill. When the Yanks won 19-8 in Boston, I had a bad feeling. I said, 'You guys just shot your load.'"

Tina had a confession, of sorts. She wasn't exactly rooting for the Red Sox in the World Series, but she wasn't rooting against them, either. This was the seventh straight season the Yankees either won the championship or lost in the playoffs to the eventual winner. That was worth something, a ceremonial second-place trophy.

"I always believed, when a team beats you, you've got to root for them," Tina said. "It was really, really, really hard for me not to root for them. The Red Sox represented the American League. I can't stand the way their players look, all scraggly, but they played the way the Yankees used to play. If they got to win once, let 'em win. I'm not mad. It's over and done with. We gave it to them. They wanted it more than we did. I'm not going to say I like it, but I'm not going to cry. We gave you one."

Tina had a final gracious message for the Boston fans up at Fenway, and for all those Red Sox heathens who ever thought to invade the hallowed plastic benches of Section 39 in the South Bronx. From the depth of her pinstriped soul and from the heart of the bleachers, her message contained two words:

"Congratulations, jackasses."